A Place to Walk

Unforgettable
walking holidays
from around
the world

Eloise Napier

A Place to Walk

Unforgettable
walking holidays
from around
the world

For my aunt, Malvina Moray

First published in 2003 by
Conran Octopus Limited
a part of Octopus Publishing Group
2–4 Heron Quays, London E14 4JP
www.conran-octopus.co.uk

British Library Cataloguing-in-Publication Data.
A catalogue record for this book is available
from the British Library.

ISBN: 1 84091 327 4

Publishing Director: Lorraine Dickey
Senior Editor: Katey Day
Assistant Editor: Sybella Marlow
Art Director: Chi Lam
Designer: Jeremy Tilston
Picture Researcher: Sian Lloyd
Production Manager: Angela Couchman

Printed in China

Contents

Introduction

Find a travel brochure, with a gorgeous picture of an empty beach, an azure sea and graceful palm trees, and stare at it for twenty minutes. Don't do anything else. Within five minutes you will probably be twitching with boredom; after twenty, you will be ready to throw the brochure into a shredding machine. As the philosopher Alain de Botton pointed out, just imagine what it would be like if you had to spend an entire week there.

Look instead at the pictures of a walking holiday: you find an infinite range of diversity, adventure and discovery. Boredom is not an option. Journeying to some of the most outstandingly beautiful places in the world, you have the chance to explore intriguing landscapes, inaccessible to cars and even horses. At some moments, an astonishing array of wildlife surrounds you; at other times you find yourself immersed in history and culture. The experience is uplifting and invigorating, and by the time you return home, you are infused with an unassailable feeling of achievement.

The diverse walks highlighted in this book provide the ultimate escape from the tedium of everyday life. However, this is walking for softies, not hard-core hikers; at the end of each day you arrive at a comfortable inn with rivers of hot water, delicious food and excellent wines. Someone else carries your luggage, handles all the administration details and even provides you with a picnic, while all you have to do is put one foot in front of the other and soak up the atmosphere. You don't have to be massively fit — some of the walks are no more than a gentle stroll. A few are quite challenging, but all of them are accessible to anyone who is mildly active. Each walk has a difficulty grading — easy, moderate, fairly strenuous and strenuous.

You can organise to do the walks yourself or, at the end of each section, you will find contact details for a company that arranges holidays broadly similar to the one described. The routes, timings and mileages may be slightly different, but the aim of A Place to Walk is not to give you a tedious blow-by-blow account of an individual trip, but rather to give you a feeling of what is out there, how you can do it and what you will gain from it.

There are only two ways to reach Juneau — by boat or by aeroplane. Perched between steep mountains and the sea, and surrounded by 4,660 sq km (1,800 sq miles) of ice field, Alaska's capital is one of the remotest and most beautifully placed cities in the world. It is also the only state capital you will ever visit that doesn't have a single road leading to it.

- Route rating: easy—fairly strenuous
- 6 days/5 nights
- Dates: from June to August

Juneau to Glacier Bay, Alaska

This area of south-east Alaska combines jaw-dropping scenery with a colourful past. Rugged, snow-capped mountains, steep-sided fjords and vertiginous baby-blue glaciers cascade down to a series of lush green valleys filled with a wealth of wildlife including black bears and grizzlies, black-tailed deer and spectacular bald eagles. The sea teems with life and is home to many species of whale, ranging from humpbacks and minke to orcas with their distinctive sinister shark-like triangular dorsal fins. Sea lions and porpoises are also common sights, and in August many of the streams and tributaries running down to the sea are heaving with spawning salmon — a fair proportion of which are gobbled up by opportunistic bears and eagles. It provides compulsive viewing.

In the late 1800s, the area played host to a series of frantic gold rushes. Thousands and thousands of gold prospectors made the hazardous journey to Juneau and on to Skagway. Many of them died in the process and very few made their fortunes, but their legacy lives on in the tenacity of latter day communities who live in places so far from anywhere that telephones, electricity and running hot water are not viable options.

In the summer months the climate is cool, 5–17°C (45–55°F), and quite often overcast. The area has seriously high rainfall, ranging from 1.5–5 m (5–16 ft), so having to endure up to 5 m (16 ft) of rain a year means the locals take a philosophical approach to the situation — they refer to the rain as 'liquid sunshine'.

From a walking point of view it means that waterproof, breathable clothes are essential. Eye masks are recommended if you are a light sleeper, as the 18 hours of summertime daylight may affect your sleeping patterns. The walking varies from relatively gentle through to quite testing — although there are always easier options. To really enjoy yourself, you ought to be fit enough to be able to walk up to five hours each day.

MIST CLOAKED MOUNTAINS SURROUND
ALASKA'S PICTURESQUE STATE CAPITAL JUNEAU

ONE OF THE MOST MEMORABLE WAYS TO VIEW THE
LANDSCAPE AROUND JUNEAU IS BY CABLE CAR

Day 1: Juneau — Herbert Glacier trail
14.5 km (9 miles), 5 hours
Alternative route 6.4 km (4 miles), 5 hours
After breakfast at the Westmark Baranof
Hotel, the day starts with a short bus ride
to the Herbert Glacier trailhead for a
relaxed walk through a picturesque forest
filled with Sitka spruce and Western
hemlock. Bunchberry, blueberry bushes
and devil's club line the path as you wind
your way towards the Herbert River, home
to beavers and assorted wildfowl. The
trees thin out and suddenly you find
yourself confronted with magnificent views
of the Herbert Glacier with its deep-blue
marbled crevasses. (The colour is caused
by enormous amounts of pressure which
compact the glacial ice so densely that
light can't penetrate it, thus turning it
blue.) This is a perfect spot in which to
have a picnic lunch before following the
trail back to Juneau.

THE HERBERT GLACIER AND THE HERBERT RIVER

Day 2: Haines to Skagway, via Seduction Point 12.8 km (8 miles), 5 hours
Alternative route 6.4 km (4 miles), 5 hours
A short but scenic flight up the Lynn Canal takes you to Haines — a small town which sits on a forested peninsula below the magnificent Cathedral Peaks of the Chilkat Mountains. Along with the spectacular scenery, Haines has the added benefit of comparatively dry weather, with a mere 1.2 m (4 ft) of rain a year. The circular trail begins at the Chilkat State Park Campground and swings between inland temperate rainforests and pristine coastline, giving you magical views of the Rainbow and Davidson Glaciers. It also provides you with ample opportunities to spot whales, seals, moose and bears.

Back in Haines you board the fast-ferry for Skagway, a tiny town created as a result of the Klondike Gold Rush of 1898. In this 'Home of the North Wind', the locals will cheerfully tell you that you'll never breathe the same air twice. Retaining much of its 19th-century charm, Skagway looks like a set from a spaghetti Western, with wooden planked sidewalks and false-fronted houses. One of the best places to stay is the Golden North Hotel, the oldest hotel in Alaska.

Day 3: Skagway to Denver Glacier 9.6 km (6 miles), 3 hours
Alternative route 4.8 km (3 miles), 3½ hours
In the 1890s, the 64 km (40 mile) White Pass Trail from Skagway to Klondike was one of the most terrifying trips that anyone could make. Determined gold rushers were told to take at least a year's supply of food with them when they attempted the journey, and in one year alone over 3,000 pack animals were driven to their deaths by desperate owners. Today the experience is somewhat less alarming, although the scenery along the route is as rugged and as memorable as ever. A train ride on the historic White Pass and Yukon Railway runs parallel to the old footpath and takes you to a forest nestling in the shadows of the massive Sawtooth Mountains. Tracking the eastern fork of the Skagway River, you follow the trail as it becomes increasingly overgrown and steepens up through the forest towards the Denver Glacier and then down again. Once the hike is finished, it's on to the train again for the short ride back to Skagway, where a visit to the Red Onion Saloon is essential. This century-old former brothel is now a lively bar complete with poker tables and a ragtime piano player.

THE WHITE PASS AND YUKON RAILWAY

BARTLETT COVE IN GLACIER BAY NATIONAL PARK

Day 4: Gustavus in Glacier Bay National Park to Bartlett Cove 8 km (5 miles), 3 hours
A beautiful morning flight over the Chilkat Mountains takes you down to Gustavus in the Glacier Bay National Park. After making your way to the park headquarters in Bartlett Cove, you follow a trail which takes you through the rainforest and out to the Bartlett River Estuary where a multitude of birdlife is always on display. Not only does the park have the world's highest concentration of tidewater glaciers (glaciers that end in the sea), but it is also home to over 200 species of bird. The route is lined with wildflowers, mushrooms and blueberry bushes, and your chances of seeing a black bear rootling about for food near the river's edge are high. If you have energy left after the walk, you could try some kayaking around the Beardslee Islands which are populated by bears, seals and bald eagles. Otherwise, you can retreat back to the comfort of the Gustavus Inn, a family-run homestead lodge which is renowned for its gourmet food. Gustavus has a population of about 400 and electricity arrived in the settlement only in the early 1980s; in some homes you still have to build a fire before there is any hot water.

Day 5: Glacier Bay cruise

Gustavus is about 64 km (40 miles) south of the nearest glacier, so the best way to appreciate the true majesty of these natural wonders is by sea. The *Spirit of Adventure*, a 220-passenger catamaran, leaves Bartlett Cove every morning at 7 o'clock for a nine-hour trip up the West Arm of the glaciers. On a clear day, the brilliance of the blue and white sheer walls of ice that face you is dazzling, and the noise when chunks of glacier fall into the sea is louder than thunder. With humpback whales, harbour seals and sea lions, along with the endless beauty of the glaciers, it is difficult to know where to look first, and by the time you return to the Gustavus Inn you will have undoubtedly shot every roll of film in your possession.

Day 6: Point Gustavus beach walk
up to 19.3 km (12 miles), 7 hours

Depending on how much time you have before your final flight back to Juneau, it is worth considering a walk along the shoreline to Point Gustavus to see the killer whales in Icy Straight. However, this is not an expedition for the faint-hearted: it is important to check out the time of high tide, as you could find yourself having to swim across the Salmon River as opposed to fording it safely at low tide. If time is tight, you can return to the Bartlett River trail and explore the tidal lagoon instead. Once back in Juneau, your appetite by this stage will probably have increased two-fold, so indulge yourself by visiting one of the best restaurants, Fiddlehead, which serves excellent vegetarian and seafood dishes.

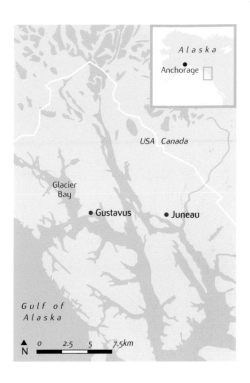

Contact: Backroads
www.backroads.com
TEL: +1 510 527 1555
FAX: +1 510 527 1444

- Route rating: moderate
- 8 days/7 nights
- Dates: December to March

Hobart to Cradle Mountain, Australia

Over two hundred million years ago, the super-continent of Gondwanaland started to break up, and the world as we know it today began to take shape. In the intervening years, dinosaurs came and went, the last great ice age petered out, and the Himalayas shot from below sea level up to heights of nearly 9,000 m (30,000 ft). In short, the world underwent a complete metamorphosis. And yet there are still one or two spots on the globe that have weathered the changes and, miraculously, look more or less the same now as they did two hundred million years ago. The most notable of these is Tasmania.

The last stopping point in the Southern Ocean before Antarctica, Tasmania lies 400 km (250 miles) south of Australia and is the country's smallest state. A remote island about the size of Ireland, it is famous for its untouched temperate wildernesses (parts of which remain unexplored to this day) and perfect beaches — one-fifth of its landmass has been declared a World Heritage Site. Its terrain is enormously varied: rugged mountains, many of which rise above 1,200 m (4,000 ft), vie with impassable rainforests; and alpine moorlands contrast with towering sea-cliffs. At times, the sea and the sky are so blue that it is difficult to tell where one ends and the other starts.

Wildlife flourishes in Tasmania — many of its trees are unique to the island, including huon pines and flowering leatherwoods. Strange-looking cushion plants, which resemble squat green stones, thrive in the high alpine areas, where weather conditions are often extreme. Marsupials are the most common indigenous mammal, and you can expect to see many examples of the infamously bad-tempered Tasmanian devil, a small, black, furry creature with a white stripe across its chest and a predilection for eating roadkill.

Although first settled by Aborigines 35,000 years ago, the majority of Tasmania's current population (473,000 people) is of British descent. Known as Van Diemen's Land, it became a notorious penal colony from 1804 to the late 1870s, and when you wander around the island's immaculately preserved Georgian houses, farms and public buildings, it is like visiting a living museum of the 19th century.

Travelling along the east coast of the island and moving to the mountainous interior, you will see some of Tasmania's most intriguing and beautiful features. However, although the summer months are warm (23°C/73°F), Tasmania is in the path of the notorious Roaring Forties, a band of wind that brings changeable weather, and as a result, strong winds and heavy rains can appear from out of the blue at any time of year, particularly in the higher regions. To cover all eventualities, take sunscreen, sunglasses and waterproof clothes.

THE FAMOUS TASMAN ARCH NEAR EAGLEHAWK NECK

BABY TASMANIAN DEVILS

THE PRISTINE RAINFORESTS OF CRADLE MOUNTAIN-
LAKE ST. CLAIR NATIONAL PARK

Day 1: Arrive in Hobart, drive to Tasman Peninsula, 1½ hours; walk from Waterfall Bay to Waterfall Bluff 4 km (2½ miles), 1½ hours; drive to Port Arthur, 20 minutes

After a morning flight into Hobart, you have the whole of the day to explore the southeastern coastline of Tasman Peninsula, joined to the mainland by a 90-m (300-ft) wide strip of land known as Eaglehawk Neck. This notorious isthmus was the last defence against convicts escaping the penal colony at Port Arthur, and a row of savage guard dogs were chained across it for many years. Having stopped to explore, and view the Tasman Arch and Devil's Kitchen blowholes, you drive to Waterfall Bay. From here you walk through slender trees on a path that hugs the coastline and passes the cascading falls of Waterfall Bluff, with their magnificent views of the bay. Once back at Waterfall Bay, it is a short drive to Port Arthur and the Port Arthur Lodge, with its luxurious waterfront cabins set among the towering gum trees.

Day 2: Wielangta Rainforest visit; drive to Orford, 15 minutes; ferry to Marie Island; hike on the island 8 km (5 miles), 3 hours

After an early start, it's a quick drive to the tall blue-gums of the Wielangta Rainforest for a half-hour meander to examine an ancient plant community which has been preserved beneath large sandstone overhangs. From here, you drive to Orford to catch the ferry for a 20-minute cruise across to Maria Island National Park. The island, with its lush forests, fern gullies, rugged limestone cliffs and immaculate beaches, is a joy to walk on. It is also home to all eleven of Tasmania's native bird species. Following a circular walk from the old township of Darlington, you reach Cape Boullanger and the Fossil Cliffs, both of which offer magnificent views across to Freycinet Peninsula and the eastern seaboard. Staying in Orford at the family-run Eastcoaster Resort, you are assured of good food and a convivial atmosphere.

**Day 3: Drive to Swansea, 1 hour;
Swansea to Waterloo Point 8 km (5 miles),
2 hours; sail to Freycinet Peninsula, 2 hours**
After arriving at Swansea, with its pretty
Georgian buildings, you follow the coastline
round a wide bay, with memorable views of
the beaches and coves of the Freycinet
Peninsula, to the small town of Coles Bay
which lies below The Hazards — three
towering 300-m (1,000-ft) outcrops. From
Coles Bay, an elegant catamaran takes you
to the secluded campsite on the peninsula.
Along the way, you may be lucky enough to
see dolphins, seals and sea eagles.

**Day 4: Freycinet National Park
11.4 km (7 miles), 4½ hours**
Famed for its stunning scenery, Freycinet
National Park is a veritable garden of Eden.
Wildflowers, including orchids, bloom in
abundance while the trees positively heave
with a huge variety of birds, including
black cockatoos and yellow-throated
honey-eaters. Climbing to the top of
Mount Graham, 570 m (1,870 ft), you will be
rewarded with perfect views of one of the
world's most isolated beaches, Wineglass
Bay. Jessie's Cottage is a most comfortable
place to stay when you return to Coles Bay.

WINEGLASS BAY

Day 5: Drive to Cradle Mountain-Lake St Clair National Park, 4 hours; walk 13 km (8 miles) of the Overland Track, 4½ hours

Cradle Mountain-Lake St Clair National Park is the most famous park in Tasmania. With its jagged dolerite ridges, thickly forested valleys, wild moorlands and glacial lakes and tarns, it is a spectacular place for walking. At the northern end of the park lies the majestic Cradle Mountain, 1,545 m (4,770 ft), with its summit crowned with cloud. Starting at Lake Dove, you follow the Overland Track through a forest and then up towards Marion's Lookout, where there is a wonderful view of Cradle Mountain reflected in the clear waters of the lake. Walking up on to a high plateau, you will see the ground dotted with alpine cushion plants and, in the distance, snow-gum trees. Making your way downhill again, along the shoulder of Barn Bluff, you arrive at the Waterfall Valley Huts, where there is basic accommodation nestled in a fabulous wilderness setting.

Day 6: Waterfall Valley to Lake Rodway via Barn Bluff Summit 11 km (7 miles), 3½ hours

This area of Tasmania is subject to mercurial weather conditions even in summer, and there is a chance you will get wet and muddy at some stage during your stay. However, it's all good fun and by the time you have reached the top of Barn Bluff — 1,559 m (5,246 ft) — the views of this remarkable area will leave you speechless with wonder. If it rains heavily, you are advised to stay on lower ground and take a trip to Lake Will for some fossil hunting. Along the way, you may find what appear to be miniature lobsters at your feet; they are actually freshwater crayfish known as 'yabbies'. As you go back past Waterfall Valley, on your way to Lake Rodway, you are almost guaranteed to see cute-looking Bennett's wallabies pottering about in the scrub nearby. Staying at the Scott Kilvert Memorial Hut at Lake Rodway, you can enjoy another peaceful night under the stars.

Day 7: Cradle Mountain circuit 6.4 km (4 miles), 3 hours

After looping round the south side of Cradle Mountain and skirting the many characteristic serrated rock formations, you make your way back down to the serene Lake Dove and the unique alpine rainforest which surrounds it. From here it is a short car ride to the sumptuous haven of Silver Ridge Lodge, a retreat beautifully positioned on the slopes of Mount Roland. After dinner, there is usually a torchlit expedition to look forward to, which takes you into the bush to spy on nocturnal marsupials — you may be able to see wombats, wallabies and possums — before returning to the lodge for the night.

Day 8: Transfer to Launceston Airport, 3 hours

THE RUGGED LANDSCAPE AS SEEN FROM THE OVERLAND TRACK IN CRADLE MOUNTAIN-LAKE ST CLAIR NATIONAL PARK

Contact: Active New Zealand
www.aussiewalkabouts.com
TEL: +64 34 41 2045

For thousands of years, the only human visitors to the Canadian Rockies were nomadic American-Indian tribes. The first intrepid Europeans arrived in the 17th century, but it was not until the 19th century that a thorough exploration and mapping of the region was instigated. This wild, impenetrable world of rugged mountains, hidden lakes and imposing glaciers attracted a certain type of visitor – hard, adventurous, determined and more than a little mad. One such infamous explorer was the Englishman Bill Peto, who arrived in Banff in 1886 and kept a permanently set bear trap in his cabin to deter burglars.

The Canadian Rockies are located in south-western Alberta and east British Columbia. Some of the most magical areas are found along a narrow belt of mountains encompassing three national parks – Banff, Yoho and Jasper. Banff is by far the most famous, with more than 25 mountains reaching altitudes of 3,000 m (9,340 ft) or more, it has been a popular spot for mountaineers, skiers and walkers since the early 1900s. It has less to offer by way of wildlife than Jasper, but in both places you should see bighorn sheep, mountain goats and eagles. Grizzly bears and cougars also populate the mountains, but you rarely see the latter. Although much larger, Jasper is more remote and consequently less visited. Yoho is the smallest park and lies adjacent to Banff.

The Rockies are subject to notoriously variable weather conditions. In the summer and early autumn the temperature can rise to 20°C (68°F), but in the winter it has been known to plummet below 0°C (32°F); cold rain and snow can descend suddenly at any time of year. As a result, it is essential always to have waterproof, windproof and breathable clothes with you so that you can be covered from head to foot should the weather change for the worse. Bringing several thin layers of under clothing, along with gloves and a warm hat, is also recommended. It is advisable to carry bottled water or purifying tablets when you are walking, as most of the streams are said to harbour giardia (a water-borne intestinal parasite, which can cause severe stomach upsets).

The Rockies – Lake Louise to Emerald Lake, Canada

- Route rating: moderate–fairly strenuous
- 8 days/7 nights
- Dates: July to September

This list of warnings makes it sound as if any trip around the Canadian Rockies is fraught with danger – it can be, but only if you fail to take precautions. With a little bit of common sense and a selection of good equipment, you will be able to savour some of the most exhilarating and memorable walking in the world, before retiring to a series of exceptionally comfortable hotels each night.

THE CANADIAN ROCKIES REFLECTED IN

THE CRYSTAL CLEAR WATERS OF EMERALD LAKE

THE VIEW FROM EMERALD LAKE LODGE

LAKE LOUISE

Day 1: Drive from Calgary to Banff
1½ hours

After the drive from Calgary airport, it is worth spending your only night in Banff at the extraordinary Banff Springs Hotel — an enormous granite building, complete with turrets and towers, which looks like a cross between a fairytale palace and a castle. The service is fabulous and staying there is an experience in itself.

Day 2: Banff National Park, Sunshine Meadows circuit 9.6 km (6 miles), 3 hours; drive to Moraine Lake Lodge

A 30-minute drive from Banff takes you past Sunshine Village Ski Resort — which at 2,215 m (7,088 ft) offers some of the best skiing in the Rockies — and finally to Sunshine Meadows. In winter the area is covered with up to 10m (32 ft) of snow, but in summer its open meadowlands flourish with wildflowers. It makes a picture-perfect setting for the start of your walk, which follows the scenic Rock Isle Trail around the eponymous lake. After a picnic lunch, see how the cragged peaks of the Monarch Range define the skyline as you join the Garden Path Trail, which takes you past Larix Lake and Simpson viewpoint. After catching the shuttlebus down the mountain, it's a 13 km (8 mile) drive up to Moraine Lake, 1,857 m (6,190 ft), to the Moraine Lake Lodge — which, with its wooden cabins, floor-to-ceiling windows and open log fires, is an impossibly romantic place to stay.

Day 3: Moraine Lake up to Larch Valley, return to Moraine Lake Lodge
17.2 km (11 miles), 6 hours

The extraordinarily vivid turquoise colour of Moraine Lake (not to mention most of the other lakes in the area) is caused by fine particles of glacial silt, known as rock flour, which absorb all shades of light apart from blue-green. The result is water of such brilliance that it looks as if it has been enhanced by computer graphics. Following a switchback trail through Larch Valley, you can appreciate this striking vision as you climb upwards to Sentinel Pass, 2,250 m (8,500 ft). It's a long slog up, but the view at the top is quite breathtaking, as the Valley of the Ten Peaks and Paradise Valley stretch out before you. If you have any energy left by the time you return to the lodge, you can hire a canoe and explore the shoreline from a different perspective.

Day 4: Moraine Lake Lodge to Lake Agnes Teahouse via Lake Louise
13.3 km (8 miles), 5 hours; short drive to Yoho National Park

Lake Louise is one of the most renowned and popular places in the Canadian Rockies. Twice the size of Lake Moraine, it attracts thousands of visitors a year, so after a quick drive down to the vast Château Lake Louise Hotel, it's best to avoid the hordes by quickly heading up towards the Victoria Glacier. You may see marmots and pika in the boulder fields along the way. The teahouse at the Plain of Six Glaciers provides a timely stop-off point for lunch before you start the 300-m (1,000-ft) climb to Lake Agnes Teahouse at 2,134 m (7,000 ft). After returning to the bustle in Lake Louise, a short drive into Yoho National Park to the 19th-century Emerald Lake Lodge will bring you back into peaceful seclusion.

EMERALD LAKE

Day 5: Yoho Valley to Emerald Lake via Yoho Pass 14.3 km (9 miles), 5 hours

When the Cree Indians wanted to express a feeling of awe or wonderment, they used the word 'yoho'. It sums up this area of the Canadian Rockies to perfection. Climbing through spruce, fir and cedar forests up a narrow switchback track from the base of Yoho Valley at 1,485 m (4,950 ft), the vistas become more and more impressive; the distant Wapta Icefield appears, along with the 254-m (813-ft) shimmering cascades of the Takakkaw Falls. After lunch at Yoho Lake — and perhaps a swim if the weather is warm enough — it's time to start the ascent to Yoho Pass, at 1,809 m (6,030 ft). Once there, you can take a breather and appreciate some more magnificent views. A slightly different route down takes you to the tranquil shores of Emerald Lake, 1,290 m (4,300 ft), from where it is a short walk back to Emerald Lake Lodge and the welcome embrace of its open log fires and delicious cuisine.

TAKAKKAW FALLS

Day 6: Wilcox Pass hike 8.8 km (6 miles), 3 hours; drive to Jasper Park Lodge

Driving northwards through Banff National Park and Icefields Parkway takes you into the remote Jasper National Park with its 1,000 km (600 miles) of trails.En route, you pass Columbia Icefields, the largest glacial area in the northern hemisphere south of the Arctic Circle; meltwater from this 325-sq-km (125-sq-mile) area runs down to the Pacific, Arctic and Atlantic oceans. The half-day hike over Wilcox Pass takes you through lush forests to a ridge with unique views over the icefields, including eight glaciers and seven of the twenty-five highest peaks in the Canadian Rockies. From here the route down leads you across beautiful meadows and beside tranquil creeks, after which it's into the car again for the journey up to Jasper Park Lodge on Lac Beauvert. This award-winning hotel is home to a championship golf course, and a swish health and beauty centre where you can have any aches and pains swiftly massaged away.

Day 7: Edith Cavell Meadows 9.6 km (6½ miles), 4 hours

The original Stoney Indian name for this mountain, inspired by its snow-capped summit bathed in moonlight, meant 'White Ghost'; Europeans renamed it after the First World War in memory of Edith Cavell, the British nurse who was executed for helping the Allies. The walk up to the 2,134-m (7,000-ft) high-point, through spruce forests, glacial moraines and wildflower-strewn alpine meadows (home to white globeflower and Indian paintbrush) is outstanding; the view at the top of Angel Glacier and the rugged north face of Mount Edith Cavell defies description. It provides a perfect climax to the walk before you descend back to Jasper Park Lodge.

Day 8: Return from Jasper National Park to Calgary

Contact: Backroads
www.backroads.com
TEL: +1 510 527 1555
FAX: +1 510 527 1444

Nova Scotia and the Fundy Isles – Digby to Wolfville, Canada

Considering the number of countries that have attempted to colonize Nova Scotia, it is staggering how sparsely populated this glorious area of Canada remains: fewer than one million people inhabit its 55,491 sq km (21,425 sq miles). Sticking out like an arm pegged on to Canada's eastern seaboard, it is surrounded by the Atlantic Ocean. Its rugged 7,400-km (4,600-mile) coastline encompasses a scenic kaleidoscope, from rolling farmland and dense woodlands to picturesque towns and wind swept boggy uplands which look as if they have come straight from the pages of J. R. R. Tolkien's *The Lord of the Rings*. It almost goes without saying that its shoreline is one of the most dramatic you will ever see.

- Route rating: easy
- 8 days/7 nights
- Dates: from June to September

The first people to inhabit Nova Scotia were the Micmac Indians, who came to the region in around 2,000 BC. Although it has been suggested that the Vikings managed to reach the province, there is little hard evidence to support this, and it is generally agreed that the first European arrival was an Englishman, John Cabot, who landed at Cape Breton in 1497. However, it was the French who established the first permanent European settlement at Port Royal in 1605, calling it Acadia. For the next 150 years, overall possession of the region alternated between the French and the British, until the latter ruthlessly expelled the Acadians in 1755. At around this time a contingent of Germans arrived as well as several thousand New Englanders, which further complicated the picture. An influx of Scots began in 1773, so tipping the ethnic balance decisively in the favour of the British. Today, this broad mix of cultures is still highly evident in the form of New England-style architecture, handmade Indian crafts, bagpipes and tartan. There are 12,500 Micmac Indians still living in the province, but the majority of the population is of British or Irish descent. The most telling of all is the fact that Nova Scotia is Latin for New Scotland.

Understandably, fishing has always played an important part in the province's economy. The seas are rich with shellfish including shrimp, lobsters and scallops, as well as fish ranging from haddock and cod to silver hake and shark. The waters that swirl in the Bay of Fundy provide an abundant food supply for many whales (finback, minke and humpback), as well as dolphins and porpoises. The area is a bird-watcher's paradise, and more than 400 species have been counted; inland, you are likely to find moose and deer.

Summer temperatures in Nova Scotia are a benign, 18–25°C (64–77°F). Be prepared for intermittent rain and wind however, and possibly fog in the morning. But, whatever the weather brings, you can be assured that nothing will dent the glorious sense of seclusion you feel as you start to explore the countryside.

COASTAL GRASSLANDS NEAR CAP LEMOINE

ON CAPE BRETON ISLAND

THE MERSEY RIVER IN KEJIMKUJIK NATIONAL PARK

Day 1: Arrive Halifax International Airport
Flight times mean that you often arrive
fairly late in Halifax so the best course
of action is to go straight to a hotel in
the city centre; Halliburton House is
Halifax's only four-star heritage inn,
and is renowned for serving some
of the region's most tempting cuisine.

**Day 2: Drive to Kejimkujik Lake, 2½ hours;
walk in Kejimkujik National Park
4.8 km (3 miles), 1½ hours; drive to Digby,
30 minutes**
One third of Nova Scotia's population lives
in Halifax, and as you drive south you
can't help but notice how few people there
are in the countryside. The scenery, once
you arrive at Kejimkujik National Park, is a
world away from that of the coastal areas.
Following a track originally used by the
Micmac Indians, you meander round
some of the lakes, bogs and forests that

characterize this region, renowned for
its wildlife. Watch out for bear and moose
which live in the depths of the park.
You will see many crested woodpeckers
in nearby trees — over 205 species of bird
have been spotted in the area, and at
night the distinctive rasp of the barred
owl is frequently heard. After the walk, a
30-minute drive takes you to the coastal
town of Digby, where the Pines Resort
Hotel offers old-world elegance, award-
winning cuisine and tremendous views
over the Annapolis Basin.

Day 3: Drive from Digby to Long Island, 1 hour; walk to Beautiful Cove 4.8 km (3 miles), 1½ hours; wildlife-watching cruise on the Bay of Fundy

Driving down the long strip of land that juts out into the Bay of Fundy, known as Digby Neck, you pass bogs and forests, as well as several small fishing villages. A 10-minute ferry ride takes you across to Long Island which is renowned for its diverse wildlife. As you make your way to Balancing Rock, you should have ample opportunity to spot some of the island's 15 varieties of orchid. The views over the surging ocean are magnificent, and prepare you for the afternoon's cruise to see some of the white-sided dolphins and humpback whales that feed in these herring- and mackerel-rich waters. If you are lucky, you may see blue, sperm and pilot whales or even rare orcas before you return to the Pines Resort Hotel for a second night.

Day 4: Drive to Annapolis Royal, 30 minutes; coastal walk 3.2 km (2 miles), 1½ hours

Calling itself 'Canada's Birthplace', Annapolis Royal, with its narrow streets and historic buildings, is one of the prettiest towns in Nova Scotia. After leaving your luggage at the delightfully named Bread & Roses Inn, it's worth driving 14 km (8.7 miles) to Port Royal Habitation to wander round a replica of the original fur trading post which was the first permanent European settlement in Canada. After this fascinating experience, head off along one of the Delaps Cove Wilderness Trails, which take you through woodland down to the rocky coastline. Once back in Annapolis Royal, going on the 9.30pm candle-lit Old Burying Ground walking tour round the ancient cemetery is not as morbid as it sounds – it actually provides an intriguing insight into Nova Scotia's history and architecture.

OLD ENGLISH ARCHITECTURE IN THE MIDDLE OF NOVA SCOTIA

FALLEN SUGA MAPLE LEAVES IN BLOMIDON

PROVINCIAL PARK

Day 5: Drive from Annapolis Royal to Blomidon Provincial Park, 1 hour; walk to Cape Blomidon 10.2 km (6 miles), 3 hours
Located at the southern tip of a spit of land that extends into the Bay of Fundy, north of Wolfville, Blomidon Provincial Park is covered by a diverse forest of striped maple, red maple and spruce. Following the Jodrey Trail, you walk along a series of imposing red cliffs with spectacular views over the Minas Basin. This is of particular interest because the Bay of Fundy (of which the Minas Basin is a tributary) has some of the highest tides in the world, rising up to 15 m (50 ft). An offshoot of this is a tidal bore, or wave, which shoots back against the current and gives the impression that the tributary river is flowing backwards. At the baronial Blomidon Inn, a former sea captain's house with graceful interiors and four-poster beds, you can relax in the dining room and enjoy some of the seafood for which Nova Scotia is famous.

Day 6: Drive to Cape Split, 30 minutes; Cape Split Trail 13 km (8 miles), 5 hours; return to Blomidon Inn

Journeying to the northern end of Cape Split, you follow a gently winding track through woods filled with maple, birch and beech trees. Violets and other wildflowers line the path as you make your way to a colourful meadow that crests the 120-m (400-ft) high cliffs. The roar of the ocean surrounds you as you stop to take in the panoramic views of the Bay of Fundy, the Minas Basin and towns as far away as Truro; it is a truly stunning sight. On your return to the Blomidon Inn in the evening you should have time to wander round the hotel's magical garden, which glows with an outstanding array of vividly flowering plants, including rhododendrons and azaleas.

Day 7: Drive to Grand Pré, walk along Minas Basin 4.8 km (3 miles), 1½ hours;

The Grand Pré National Historic Site consists of beautiful landscaped grounds forming a memorial to the Acadians (descendents of the original French settlers) ousted by the English in 1755. This hardworking community had transformed the marshes around their settlement into productive farmland by building a series of ingenious dykes. Walking along the mudflats of the Minas Basin, you have the opportunity to inspect modern versions of the dykes which still protect the farmland from the ravages of salt water. Your final night is spent back at the Blomidon Inn.

Day 8: Return to Halifax International Airport

Contact: Backroads
www.backroads.com
TEL: +1 510 527 1555
FAX: +1 510 527 1444

Patagonia – Lake Viedma to Torres del Paine National Park, Chile/Argentina

Big feet are said to be the inspiration behind the name Patagonia. When the Portuguese adventurer Ferdinand Magellan, who coined the name, first explored this remote region of South America in the early 16th century, he found that the indigenous tribespeople, the Tehuelche, wore huge moccasins filled with insulating grass to protect their feet from frostbite, known as *patagones* – hence Patagonia. Whether this is true or not, it is a delightful story about an area of the world that has fascinated travellers for generations.

• Route rating: moderate–fairly strenuous
• 8 days/7 nights
• Dates: December to March

Embracing the southern ends of both Chile and Argentina (about one-third of the land area of each country), Patagonia is more a state of mind than a specific geographical area – there is no formalized border as such, just a general agreement that it starts somewhere around the Río Biobío in Chile and Río Colorado in Argentina, and stretches all the way south to Tierra del Fuego. The landscape varies extravagantly – the Chilean strip encompasses impenetrable forests and some of the wettest terrain in the world, while much of the Argentinian section is composed of a broad, semi-barren plateau – so monotonous that Charles Darwin observed, 'The curse of sterility is on the land.' However, where these two distinct regions meet, in the Patagonian Andes, the landscape erupts into a smorgasbord of massive glaciers, jagged snow-capped mountains, vivid blue lakes and desolate pampas. It is an area so remote, so unspoilt and so sparsely populated that if it were divided up into small parts there would only be one person living on each square kilometre of land.

Southern Patagonia contains the highest concentration of glaciers in South America, and is one of the most beautiful places you will ever visit. Stretching from the Península de Taitao and Lake Carrera to the Straits of Magellan, it includes the world famous Torres del Paine and Los Glaciares National Parks. Unsurprisingly, its range of flora and fauna is extensive. Rare Andean condors soar like giant tea-trays high above, while yellow bridled finches flit among the trees in the lowland valleys. Furry aquatic coypus, similar to beavers, populate freshwater areas, and native foxes patrol the landscape.

The climate of southern Patagonia is typified by strong winds and sudden storms, interspersed with lulls of fine, stable weather. In the summer months (mid-December to mid-March) daytime temperatures can rise to 24–27°C (75–80°F). Because the region lies under an area of depleted ozone, combined with dry, unpolluted air, the risk of sunburn is severe. A broad-brimmed hat, sunglasses (to avoid the damaging glare in glacial areas) and sunscreen are essential items of equipment, along with warm and waterproof clothing. If you wear contact lenses, it is advisable to bring glasses with you to avoid possible irritation caused by sand or dust being blown into your eyes by the wind.

LAKE ROCA IN CALAFATE ROCA INTERNATIONAL RESERVE

Day 1: Fly from Buenos Aires to El Calafate, 3 hours; drive to Lake Viedma, 3½ hours
The scenery along the drive from El Calafate to Lake Viedma is typically variable, ranging from harsh, rolling steppes to beech forests and on to the snow-capped, needle-sharp summits of the El Chaltén Range. Arriving at the remote Hostería Helsingfors, on the shores of Lake Viedma, you have time to wander along the water's edge and take in the views of the imposing granite pinnacles of Monte Fitz Roy, 3,460 m (11,355 ft), and Cerro Torre, 3,146 m (10,322 ft), before returning to the hotel (which doubles as a working ranch) for dinner. Food-wise, you can expect to be offered substantial quantities of red meat — Argentina is famed for its steaks, although there are other options including fresh trout, chicken or pasta.

Day 2: Lake Viedma to Laguna Azul
17.7 km (11 miles), 4 hours

Hostería Helsingfors is situated at the
northern end of the Los Glaciares National
Park, a vast tract of wilderness which was
declared a World Heritage Site in 1982.
Leaving Lake Viedma, you make your way
through windswept pampas to the forested
foothills of the Fitz Roy sector. A gradual
295-m (968-ft) climb takes you to Laguna
Azul – the Blue Lagoon – surrounded by
towering mountains and fed by a dazzlingly
white hanging glacier. Along the way you
will be able to spot many examples of the
ubiquitous calafate bush, with its bright
yellow flowers in spring and contrasting
purple berries in late summer and early
autumn. Back down at Hostería Helsingfors,
you have a free afternoon in which to relax.

Day 3: Boat cruise to Viedma Glacier,
2½ hours; walk along Lake Viedma
16 km (10 miles), 3½ hours

A 60-seater launch, the *Huemul*, leaves
Helsingfors to take you to the massive
Viedma Glacier, where you can watch
icebergs floating gently in the waters
nearby. The *Huemul* then glides along
the western side of the lake, affording
tremendous views of the surrounding
countryside. In the afternoon, an optional
walk along the lake should give you a
chance to see some of the park's
multifarious birdlife, including austral
blackbirds, grey-hooded finches, torrent
ducks and possibly a forest owl. Keen
equestrians can borrow a horse from
the nearby ranch and take a guided ride
across the pampas, where they may
catch sight of the rare Patagonian hare,
the mara, or even an armadillo.

Day 4: Drive to Perito Moreno via
El Calafate, 3½ hours

Leaving Lake Viedma, you make your
way slowly (the road condition is not
great) to Lake Argentino, Argentina's
largest lake, with a surface area of
1,600 sq km (618 sq miles). El Calafate
is a small, fairly unmemorable town
filled with tourist shops, (however, it
does have ATM machines if you are
running short of cash). Continuing
southwest, you arrive at Hostería Los
Nostros, a delightful country lodge
with magnificent views of the
staggering Perito Moreno Glacier.

JAGGED MOUNTAINS AND WILDFLOWERS IN
TORRES DEL PAINE NATIONAL PARK

Day 5: Boat ride across Brazco Rico, 20 minutes; guided walk on Perito Moreno Glacier 6.4km (4 miles), 2 hours

A short boat trip across the Brazco Rico, an arm of Lake Argentino, takes you past the Canal de los Témpanos (Iceberg Channel) to the shore alongside the Perito Moreno Glacier. At 60 m (200 ft) high and 4.8 km (3 miles) wide, this is one of the world's greatest natural wonders. One of only two advancing glaciers in South America, it provides spectators with a fabulous floorshow: you will see huge pieces of ice — weighing several thousands of kilograms — rip away from the glacier face and crash down to the waters below. The noise is like cannon fire and the colour of the exposed ice ranges from bright white to deep blue. Attaching crampons to your feet, you follow the footsteps of a guide across the ice, past crevasses and jagged ice obelisks. This is not as strenuous as it sounds, although you are well advised to wear warm, windproof clothes. Back at Hostería Los Nostros, you can expect some delicious traditional cuisine at dinner, including rolled lamb with rosehip sauce or beef *parrillas*.

Day 6: Drive across the continental divide from Argentina to Chile, 5 hours; afternoon hike from Lake Pehoé to Mirador Condor 8 km (5 miles), 2 hours

After driving through a seemingly never-ending stretch of windswept pampas, you arrive at the luxurious wilderness resort of Explora, nestling on the shores of Lake Pehoé in the Torres del Paine National Park. If you are feeling self-indulgent after your long drive, you can opt for a massage or a swim in the pool. Otherwise there is a steep afternoon climb to Mirador Condor, from where the views of the surrounding serrated granite peaks are excellent. You should also have the opportunity to see some of the park's multifarious wildlife, including guanacos (similar to llamas) and grey foxes.

Day 7: Guided trek to Campamento Británico 24 km (15 miles), 6 hours

This is the most strenuous day of the trip (although there are other more leisurely options available). It is advisable to wear long trousers, as after hiking through a lenga (southern beech tree) forest, you climb a steep trail with thorny calafate bushes on either side as you make your way along to the Vallé Francés.

After scrambling across a boulder-strewn moraine, you reach the Campamento Británico. From here, weather permitting, there are panoramic views of the mountains – Paine Grande, 3,050 m (10,010 ft), towering in the west and Alta del Tiburon (the Shark's Fin) to the north. In the distance, you can see Explora at the far end of Lake Pehoé. Back at the hotel, you will be more than ready to collapse into the embrace of the outdoor hot tub.

Day 8: Drive to Punta Arenas, 7 hours, to catch a connecting flight to Santiago.

WALKING UP TOWARDS MIRADOR CONDOR IN TORRES DEL PAINE NATIONAL PARK

Contact: Backroads
www.backroads.com
TEL: +1 510 527 1555
FAX: +1 510 527 1444

What do you do if hordes of barbarians keep attacking your farms, stealing your livestock and running off with your women? If you are Offa, King of the Mercians (757–796AD), you build a large earthen embankment with a stockade on the top, stretching from one edge of your kingdom to the other, and hope that it will be enough to keep the marauders penned into their own territory.

- Route rating: moderate
- 7 days/7 nights
- Dates: all year round

Offa's Dyke – Chepstow to Knighton, England

This happened in the 8th century and for many years the 240-km (150-mile) embankment marked the border between England and Wales. Longer than Hadrian's Wall, which was built to mark England's northern boundary, and the Antonine Wall, situated between the Clyde and Forth rivers, put together, its construction was an extraordinary achievement, and some historians have described it as one of the greatest public works in Europe of its time. Over twelve hundred years later, at least 128 km (80 miles) of Offa's Dyke (as it has come to be known) still remain, in the form of ditches and banks which stretch intermittently through the counties of Gloucestershire, Gwent, Hereford and Worcester, Powys and Clywd.

A path has been established that broadly follows the route of the dyke as it winds from Chepstow on the Severn Estuary up to Prestatyn on the Irish Sea coast of north Wales. The route takes you through a broad spectrum of landscapes, from river flatlands and low-lying oak forests to heathland and moorland. Along the way, you pass ruined castles and abbeys, ancient hill forts and medieval churches. You also have ample opportunity to spot a broad cross-section of British wildlife, from wild Welsh mountain ponies and foxes to hedgehogs and grey squirrels. For much of the way, the patchwork quilt of hedge-lined fields is dotted with sheep and dairy cattle.

The climate in Britain is variable and it is quite possible to experience three different season's worth of weather — heavy rain, hail and bright sunshine — in the space of one afternoon.

As with most countries, the higher the altitude the greater the chance of sudden (and possibly extreme) weather changes; it is sensible to have waterproof and windproof clothing wherever you are walking in Britain. Generally, the Offa's Dyke path can be walked throughout the year (if there is snowfall in winter, it usually doesn't lie for long), but daytime temperatures can drop to -1°C (30°F) from mid-winter to mid-spring, with an average high of 21°C (70°F) in summer.

To fit the trip into a week, this version of the Offa's Dyke path concentrates on the southern section, from Chepstow to Knighton; to keep the wind and the sun mainly on your back, it is best to travel from south to north. You need to be fit to complete this walk: although it is not desperately steep, the days are long and there are numerous stiles to climb.

TINTERN ABBEY IN GWENT

Day 1: Chepstow

It is easy to reach Chepstow by car, coach or rail (services from London Paddington via Newport). Afon Gwy, a comfortable bed and breakfast (B&B) with a good dining room, is an ideal place to spend the first night as it is conveniently situated close to the beginning of the walk. If you have time, visit Chepstow's castle, built in 1067 and the first major stone fortification to be constructed in Wales.

SUMMER SUN FILTERS THROUGH A
TREE-LINED AVENUE IN THE WYE VALLEY

Day 2: Chepstow to Redbrook
22.4 km (14 miles), 5½ hours

The route starts at Sedbury Cliffs, with the mudflats below and views across the River Severn estuary. Winding through Chepstow, you pass the castle and walk out towards open countryside. With limestone cliffs dropping down to the River Wye on your left, you come to Wintour's Point – named after a Royalist soldier who is said to have leapt down the 60-m (200-ft) cliffs to escape his Parliamentarian pursuers during the English Civil War (1642–1646). Climbing high above the Wye Valley, you arrive at Shorn Cliff to be presented with a magnificent view of the 14th-century Tintern Abbey. Walking towards these awe-inspiring ruins, you reach an isolated limestone outcrop known as the Devil's Pulpit, from where, according to legend, Satan preached in an attempt to corrupt the monks at Tintern. Continuing along the river through woods and farmland, you eventually head down to the village of Redbrook, where the Old Brewery, a recommended B&B, lies close to The Bell, a popular gastro-pub.

Day 3: Redbrook to Llanvetherine
26 km (16 miles), 7 hours

Climbing up through more farmland you soon reach the Naval Temple and Round House viewpoint. If the weather is good, the views are stupendous and you can even see the Black Mountains in the far distance. Next you walk to the ancient town of Monmouth, where there is time for a quick coffee before heading up through the boggy King's Wood. In 17.7 km (11 miles) you will come to the moated 12th-century White Castle, one of the highlights of the day. From here it is a 20 minute walk into Llanvetherine and Brook Cottage B&B, which serves organic breakfasts and provides transport for dinner to the Walnut Inn, renowned for its delicious food.

Day 4: Llanvetherine to Longtown
19.3 km (12 miles), 6½ hours

After leaving Brook Cottage you follow the trail to Llangattock-Lingoed and Pandy, where you leave the lowland farms and climb onto Hatterrall Ridge, part of the Black Mountains and the easternmost point of the Brecon Beacons National Park. Although the views are impressive the countryside is bleak, with few trees and little shelter, so it is a relief to make your way down towards Longtown and Olchan Court B&B, a charming 14th-century converted farmhouse complete with four-poster beds.

THE BRECON BEACONS

Day 6: Hay-on-Wye to Kington
23.5 km (14½ miles), 7½ hours

This is a day filled with contrasts. Starting by crossing the River Wye, you follow the undulating track through arable land into the Radnorshire Hills. After Newchurch, you start to climb up into moorland, past Hill Farm (which has a drinking water tap with a sign attached declaring, 'It's cool, it's fresh, it's free!') and on to the small pub in Gladestry, which is perfect for lunch. Bear in mind, however, that there is a steep climb afterwards to Hergest Ridge. Wild thyme and gorse line the path, while Welsh mountain ponies graze on the slopes nearby. Walking down through the bracken, you arrive at the small Saxon town of Kington, where the 700-year-old Penrhos Court Country House Hotel is the best place to stay. Voted 'Restaurant of the Year' by the Soil Association Organic Food Awards, you are assured of delicious cuisine.

Day 5: Longtown to Hay-on-Wye
23.5 km (14½ miles), 7½ hours

After a hearty breakfast, the climb back up to Hatterrall Ridge is a bit of a shock, but once you are up there the fresh air clears your head pretty quickly. After walking over the Cat's Back, you make your way to the highest point of the path, at 703 m (2,306 ft). At this stage the path widens out and becomes quite peaty and, when wet, fairly boggy. There is often low cloud over the mountains which can be extremely disorientating, so it is important to take a compass and a map. The walk along the ridge ends at Hay Bluff and, weather allowing, you should be able to see Hay and the Wye Valley, the Black Mountains, the Brecon Beacons and the Radnorshire Hills. A steep descent, through five kissing gates, takes you into the delightful town of Hay-on-Wye, made famous by its 30 second hand book shops and its annual literary festival. The Bear, a B&B in a quaint 17th-century house in the town centre, is a convenient and comfortable place to stay.

Day 7: Kington to Knighton
22 km (14½ miles), 7½ hours

This is quite a tiring day, as you travel through hill country which grows steeper the further north you venture. You walk next to Offa's Dyke for most of the way and pass England's highest golf course at Bradnor Hill. By this stage, the Dyke reaches 5–7 m (16–23 ft) in height and the panoramic views of the Brecon Beacons and the Malvern Hills are outstanding. Descending to the market town of Knighton, you can spend your final night in the comfort of the three-star Knighton Hotel.

FAN Y BIG IN THE BRECON BEACONS

Contact: Sherpa Expeditions
www.sherpaexpeditions.com
TEL: +44 (0)20 8577 2717
FAX: +44 (0)20 8572 9788

For centuries the hills of the Cévennes have provided an ideal haven for hermits, exiles and those of a generally rebellious nature. A relatively inaccessible and sparsely populated area of France, characterized by thick forests, rugged hills and mountains, it was and remains to this day an ideal place in which to escape. Forming an outcrop running south and west of the Massif Central, it is also known as the Haut Languedoc.

TRADITIONAL FARMHOUSE EN ROUTE TO LE VIGAN

The Cévennes – Le Vigan to Millau, France

- Route rating: fairly strenuous
- 8 days/7 nights
- Dates: from May to September

The beauty of this unspoilt area was most famously described by Robert Louis Stevenson in his book *Travels with a Donkey*, which chronicles his 192-km (120-mile) journey in 1878 from one side of the Cévennes to the other with a temperamental ass called Modestine. He was drawn to the area by blood-soaked stories he had read of the 18th-century persecution of local Protestants, or Camisards, who fought a bitter guerrilla war against their Catholic oppressors from hiding places in the region's myriad gorges and caves. Five centuries earlier, the Cathars had concealed themselves in those very same hiding places to escape the terrors of the Inquisition.

In the intervening years the landscape has changed little. Much of it has been turned into a National Park (the second largest in France) where no chemical spraying is allowed. The park teems with wildlife and 1,600 plant, 208 bird and 89 mammal species. Beavers, deer (both red and roe), griffon, black vultures and even capercaillie are common sights.

The walking here is exceptionally varied. Following ancient mule tracks and drovers' roads, you pass through rolling pastures covered by carpets of wildflowers, up into high forested hills and down to dramatic gorges and subterranean caverns. In July and August the temperature can rise to 28°C (85°F), but by September it drops to about 17°C (65°F) It rains rarely, so only the lightest of waterproof clothing is necessary, sunscreen however, is essential. Although most of the route is marked with GR way marks (*grande randonnée* – the French system of graded footpaths), taking detailed maps with you is recommended.

PANORAMIC VIEW OF THE UPPER LANGUEDOC

Day 1: Drive from Marseille airport to Le Vigan 2½ hours

On the journey from the airport it is worth stopping to visit the historic town of Montpellier, which is renowned for its beautiful architecture; its cathedral and museums are of particular interest. From here it is not far to Pont d'Hérault, a small hamlet close to Le Vigan. Before retiring to the family-run Château du Rey back in Pont d'Hérault for the night, you should have time to explore Le Vigan, with its fine medieval bridge, pretty chestnut trees and museum which provides a fascinating insight into the regions history including local crafts and geology. In the last century, the area was an important centre of silk production, and today you can still see many of the original mulberry trees which were planted to provide the leaves used to feed the precious silkworms.

Day 2: Le Vigan to L'Espérou 18.2 km (11 miles), 5½ hours

Following a path up through the chestnut, pine and beech woods above Le Vigan, you come out onto a high ridge with excellent views of the Arre and Hérault valleys. The first two hours of this walk are fairly strenuous as you make your way up past the village of Beaulieu and then on to the Col de la Lusette, at 1,269 m (4,162 ft): bring some warm clothes as the temperature will fluctuate as you get higher. The views of the Cévennes are spectacular, and along the way you should see lavender, mint, and purple-winged and elder-flowered orchids. Following a drover's track through Aigoual Forest, you arrive at the mountain village of L'Espérou. The best place to stay is at the Hôtel du Parc, where you can sample traditional home cooking, including wild boar and *tartes aux myrtilles*.

Day 3: L'Espérou to Prat Peyrot circuit 16 km (10 miles), 4½ hours

L'Espérou is in the middle of the Cévennes National Park and it is a good idea to spend one day exploring the area. Making your way to the ski station at Prat Peyrot (the area is well known for cross-country skiing in the winter), you then follow the signs to Croix de Fer. Along the way you will see the Causse Méjean, one of the Cévennes' great upland plateaux — barren wastelands clothed with almost nothing save bleached grass, thistles and occasional orchids. From Col de la Sérréyrède, you make your way back down to L'Espérou. This area is a botanist's paradise, and the edges of the paths are dotted with star-of-Bethlehem, five-leaved coralwort and forget-me-nots.

THE RIVER HERAULT

Day 4: L'Espérou to Meyrueis
17.7 km (11 miles), 6½ hours

This day's walk follows the well-signed GR6a and GR6b routes closely, so you won't need to rely as heavily as usual on your maps to find your way down to Meyrueis, 699 m (2,330 ft). En route, you will find hellebores, soapwort and pasque flowers in the vegetation. You may also be able to hear — and possibly even see — cuckoos, skylarks and wagtails in the trees above. The night is spent at a 12th-century converted Benedictine monastery, the Château d'Ayres.

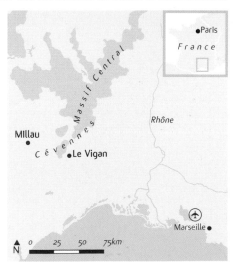

Day 5: Meyrueis to Aven Armand circuit
10.4 km (6½ miles), 3 hours

The walk out of Meyrueis up to the Causse Méjean is steep but very beautiful. Once on the limestone plateau, you will pass the Tombe du Géant — a large, prehistoric menhir somewhere between four thousand and five thousand years old. A short distance from here is Aven Armand, a complex of caves said to have the 'finest stalagmite formations in Europe'. They are fascinating to see, although not recommended if you suffer from claustrophobia. Back in Meyrueis, you can use any spare time to go horse riding (which can be organized at the Château), or just soak up the atmosphere as you wander through the old, twisting streets lined with 16th-century houses. It is an ideal time to sample some of the delicious local delicacies, which include chanterelles, truffles, Roquefort cheese and wines from Gaillac.

Day 6: Aven Armand to Le Rozier
20.8 km (13 miles), 6 hours

This is a day to bring binoculars with you, as the views are out of this world. After a short drive to Aven Armand, you make your way through open countryside up to the villages of Les Hérans, Hielzas and the fortified hamlet of Les Bastides. More often than not, you will see vultures soaring in the skies above, and in spring there is a profusion of colourful wildflowers. Following the path, you arrive at the village of St Pierre des Tripiers with its exquisite 10th-century Romanesque church. After lunch, you begin the journey down to Le Rozier, which is fairly steep and at times quite hard going. However, the views of the Tarn and Jonte gorges are well worth suffering any momentary aches and pains caused by the 750-m (2,500-ft) descent. The Grand Hôtel de la Muse et du Rozier sits at the water's edge in the Tarn Gorge, and is a comfortable place to stay.

Day 7: Le Rozier to Millau
22.4 km (14 miles), 7½ hours

This is probably the most gruelling day of the trip. Climbing from about 450 m (1,500 ft) up to 1,200 m (4,000 ft), you make your way to the Causse Noir, a plateau above the Tarn and Jonte gorges. Again, there are ample opportunities for plant spotting and you may see lily-of-the-valley, dwarf daphne, giant Canterbury bells and Solomon's seal along the route. From the village of Le Maubert, follow the GR62 to Millau, a medium-sized town situated in a bowl below the cliffs of the Tarn and Dourbie gorges. A well-known glove-making centre in the 12th century, Millau was also a medieval place of pilgrimage thanks to a thorn from the Crown of Thorns that was said to belong to the Church of Notre Dame de L'Espinasse, which still stands today. La Musardière, an attractive hotel in the centre of the town, serves excellent food and has 14 elegant bedrooms.

LOOKING OVER THE TARNON VALLEY FROM THE CAUSSE MEJEAN

THE IMPOSING JONTE GORGE

Day 8: Return to Marseille airport, 3 hours
If you have time before your return flight, try to visit Graufesenque, an archaeological site dating from Roman times situated about 0.8 km (½ mile) south of Millau.

Contact: ATG Oxford
www.atg-oxford.co.uk
TEL: +44 (0)1865 315 678
FAX: +44 (0)1865 315 697

There is a small corner of Greece that remains stubbornly impervious to the onslaughts of 21st-century tourism, and is still free from the hoards of lobster-hued sun-worshippers, droves of earnest classical scholars and enthusiastic yachties who invade the rest of the country every summer. Zagoria, hidden away in the Pindos Mountains just south of the border with Albania, is one of Europe's last true wildernesses. Rugged peaks, boulder-strewn ravines, hallucinogenic lunar landscapes and vertiginous cliffs characterize its extraordinarily varied scenery.

- Route rating: fairly strenuous
- 8 days/7 nights
- Dates: from May to October

Paths of the Pindos – Monodendri to Ioánnina, Greece

Fittingly, the Slavic word *zagoria* means 'the land behind the mountains', and it is this inaccessibility that has historically given the local population a remarkable degree of autonomy. Uniquely, under Ottoman rule Greek culture still managed to flourish here. During the Second World War it was the heartland of the resistance fighters. The collection of 46 villages which make up the district is known as the Zagorohoria. These medieval stone-built settlements, with cobbled streets and stone-tiled roofs, cling to the sides of precipitous mountains, and are inhabited by a dwindling population. Life in some of the remote villages has hardly changed in centuries; Vlach shepherds, who migrate up to the summer pastures each year, still speak a Latin-based language used by their ancestors 2000 years ago.

Surprisingly for such an under-populated area there is relatively little wildlife, which is mainly thanks to the Greek's love of hunting. However, you will see numerous raptors, including Egyptian vultures and golden eagles. Occasionally you may be lucky enough to spy a fox, a deer or a hare; brown bears, lynxes and wolves are known to live in the area, but your chances of seeing them are remote. Flowers, on the other hand, are everywhere – violets, gentians and lizard orchids flourish in June, while cyclamen bloom in October.

The temperature rises to 27°C (80°F) in July and August, and although it is usually sunny, the weather conditions become more unpredictable the higher you go, so it is advisable to have something light and waterproof with you at all times. Life in this remote region has its own pace – and that is slow; there are few banks, no cash dispensers and hardly any shops. Service in some of the places you stay may be slightly eccentric, but what your hosts lack in slickness, they more than make up for in generosity and charm.

THE SHEPHERDS' BRIDGE AT KIPI

Day 1: Drive from Ioánnina to Vitsa, 1 hour
Flight times mean that you usually arrive in Ioánnina, the one-time capital of the 19th-century Albanian tyrant Ali Pasha, too late for any sightseeing. However, a short drive takes you up through the wooded foothills of the Gamila massif, where wild pear trees and poplars sprout from the rock-strewn earth, to the Zagorian village of Vitsa. Your first night is spent at the Selini Hotel — a simple but comfortable resting place with excellent views. As with virtually all the places you will stay in the area, you should not expect televisions or direct-dial telephones.

THE MAGNIFICENT VIKOS GORGE

Day 2: Monodendri to Kipi
10.8 km (6½ miles), 4½ hours

After breakfast, a brief drive up a steep winding road takes you to Monodendri, a village which is architecturally almost indistinguishable from Vitsa — narrow, cobbled mule tracks run between stone walls and roofed gates, which enclose small houses with stone tiles. Almond trees arch over the pavements, scattering blossom in the spring. A ten-minute walk from the village square brings you to a shelf of rock from which you can look down the vertical cliffs of the Vikos Gorge. Over the sound of the gushing river, you can hear the hum of thousands of bees drifting up from the ravines below. Suspended on a small promontory above the gorge is the 15th-century monastery of Agia Paraskevi, now abandoned. After exploring this and the hermit's cave nearby, make your way down the paved path to the gorge and follow the riverside path upstream. You will need to cross narrow sections of the river four times, so bring some spare shoes with you. The track becomes a road and leads you to Kipi, a hamlet set in the midst of a green valley. Staying in the traditional Artemis Guest House and eating at a nearby taverna will give you a taste of authentic local life.

Day 3: Kipi to Tsepelovo
9 km (5½ miles), 3 hours

Although the walk today is relatively short, it is important to leave early in the morning so as to complete the initial uphill stage before the day's heat sets in. Once above the village, you will enjoy excellent views of Mount Gamila, 2,497 m (8,100 ft), before dropping back down into the Vikakis Valley, where you cross one of the region's many elegant stone bridges. Built in the 18th century, these bridges were essential for shepherds to move their flocks safely over the swollen rivers. A final steep track takes you up to the largest of the Zagorian villages, Tsepelovo, where you will stay at the Drakolimini Hotel.

Day 4: Tsepelovo to Astrakas refuge
17.9 km (11 miles), 7 hours

This is the hardest day's walking, but the most rewarding. It is essential to get up early as the first couple of hours are uphill. The track takes you high into the Gamila Mountains, with alpine meadows and a few isolated shepherd's huts en route. The total climb is over 800 m (2,600 ft), although as this is spread over 17.9 km (11 miles), it feels less exhausting than it sounds. You will eventually reach the Astrakas refuge, a simple building set into the side of the mountain with dormitory-style accommodation and superb views. This is your chance to experience the high-mountain pastoral life that has existed in the Balkans for centuries.

Day 5: Astrakas refuge to Mirko Papingo
18.8 km (11½ miles), 6 hours

Perched on the edge of a mountain overlooking a hair-raising drop down to the Aoos Gorge is Drakolimni (Lake Dragon), so called because of the alpine newts that lurk in its waters. A 90-minute walk from the refuge across grassy hillsides brings you to this magnificent spot, which provides a perfect stop for lunch; after this you turn back for the two-hour walk to the picturesque village of Mirko Papingo, used by the Sarakatsanis shepherds as their winter retreat. Cobbled passages (too narrow for cars) and almond trees intersperse the small, rather squat houses, while over 1,000 m (3,270 ft) above them the castellated cliffs of the Gamila Mountains tower skywards. One of the most delightful places to stay is the Dias Pension, where you can enjoy a delicious dinner including local cheeses, stuffed vine leaves and lamb stew.

Day 6: Mirko Papingo to Aristi
13 km (8 miles), 4½ hours

A small path through woods filled with holm oaks, horse chestnuts and Judas trees takes you down to the heart of the savagely beautiful Vikos Gorge, with the fang-like Gamila summits disappearing behind you. After two hours you reach the gorge bottom to be confronted by the extraordinary sight of the Voidomatis River, which wells up from nowhere, fed by icy underground springs. It is a remarkably tranquil spot, ideal for a lunch stop, before you start the hot hour-long ascent up to the village of Vitsiko. From here there is a fairly flat walk along a winding minor road until you reach Aristi. At the Zisis Hotel you are assured of a lively welcome by the three brothers who run it. The food they serve is delicious, but the portion sizes are enormous so be careful not to over-order.

Greece

• Monodendri

Athens •

✈ Ioánnina

• Dodona

Arahthos

Ionian Sea

0   15   30   45km

N

Day 7: Aristi to Kleidonia
14.8 km (9 miles), 5 hours; drive to Ioánnina, 1 hour

Walking back down to the banks of the Voidomatis on a new track, you pass the dramatic Spiliotissa monastery hugging a rocky outcrop above the river. For years it has remained uninhabited but, a restoration programme has been implemented to turn it back into a working monastic community. The surrounding plane tree forest is strikingly photogenic, but don't be beguiled by its beauty if you suffer from hay fever – its pollen count goes off the scale. An optional short walk upstream will reveal orchids and butterflies in the fertile pastures adjacent to the river. Heading back downstream again on a somewhat overgrown path (beware of the ankle-high thistles), you will pass a series of caves which were first inhabited by man over 33,000 years ago. Crossing another of the regions characteristic elegantly arched stone bridges, you enter the hamlet of Kleidonia. From here it is a minibus ride back to Ioánnina and the bustle of urban life. The Hotel Kastro provides a good place to stay in the town's historic centre.

Day 8: Ioánnina to Dodona

If flight times permit, try to visit the ancient Greek shrine of Dodona, which is mentioned by both Homer and Hesiod. The remains of a theatre built c.274BC to seat 17,000 people can still be seen today.

THE AMPHITHEATRE AT DODONA

Contact: ATG Oxford
www.atg-oxford.co.uk
TEL: +44 (0)1 865 315 678
FAX: +44 (0)1 865 315 697

When the mist rises out of the valleys, wrapping thousands of verdant trees in a diaphanous shroud, the locals in the Black Forest smile and say quietly, 'The witches are brewing up their coffee again.'

- Route rating: easy
- 8 days/7 nights
- Dates: from May to October

The Black Forest – Triberg to Vöhrenbach, Germany

In the southwestern tip of Germany, sandwiched between France and Switzerland, the Black Forest stretches for 170 km (106 miles) from Karlsruhe in the north to Basle in the south. This densely wooded area echoes with legend and has a distinctive local culture which has been shaped by a romantic and colourful history. Described by the Germans as *Mittelgebirge* (which basically means middle-ranking hills – not big enough to be described as mountains, but definitely more than hills), it has been a popular walking destination for many generations. Never rising above 1,500 m (4,500 ft), it provides gentle exercise combined with panoramic views. You do not have to be super-fit, but good stamina is a must.

The Black Forest is made up of not just one forest but a series and is characterized by two distinct types of landscape: in the north, moorland, heathland and vineyards; in the south, dramatic woodlands and scattered farms. Despite their popularity, the woods are remarkably unspoilt and abound with flora and fauna, including black squirrels, wild boar and over 3,000 species of butterfly.

In the 19th century, the Black Forest was the capital of the world's cuckoo clock-making industry, and although global demand for cuckoo clocks has since declined, the area is still famed for its skilled carpenters and furniture-makers. The Clock Carriers' Way broadly follows the paths that the artisans travelled 200 years ago, and the trail is usually marked by a sign depicting a red and white clock face on a white background (Unfortunately, the signs are rather pretty and are frequently swiped, so it is important not to rely on them.)

The best months for walking in the Black Forest are May and September. In July and August temperatures rise to over 27°C (80°F), which can make walking uncomfortable. October is the most spectacular time to visit, as the leaves begin to change colour and in parts of the forest it feels as if you are walking through a golden cathedral. However, sudden storms are possible throughout the year so it is important to always take something warm and waterproof with you. Travelling with a picnic is usually unnecessary, as a series of inns dotted throughout the forest are guaranteed to provide outstanding food and drink.

THE GUTACH FALLS AT TRIBERG

Day 1: Triberg

This charming town lies in the heart of the Black Forest, surrounded by pine-covered hills. The most popular place to stay is the 18th-century Romantik Parkhotel Wehrle — replete with oak panelling, antique furniture — which is renowned for its award-winning food. (On request, the hotel will arrange to pick you up from Stuttgart airport.)
If you have time, try and visit the excellent Black Forest Museum, which will give you a vivid insight into the local culture.

Day 2: Triberg to Neueck
19 km (11½ miles), 5½ hours

You have a long walk ahead of you today, so it is best to start early. The trip begins in Triberg at the base of the Gutach Falls which, at 162 m (531 ft), are the highest waterfalls in the country. It's a stiff climb through the forest to the top of the falls, but the amusing antics of the black squirrels in the boughs above you usually succeed in taking your mind off any aching muscles. After a 90-minute walk, during which you pass the small peaty lake at Blindensee, you arrive at the 13th-century St Martin's Chapel. Near by, you can visit an 18th-century farmhouse to see demonstrations on how the famous Black Forest ham is traditionally made. After sampling this delicacy, follow the rocky path up to the summit of Brend, 1,149 m (3,769 ft). Stop for a rewarding break to enjoy the stunning views before rejoining the path and making your way down to the family-run two-star hotel in Neueck.

Day 3: Neueck to St Märgen
14 km (8½ miles), 4 hours

The day starts with a gentle walk past meadows and forests filled with wild irises, turk's-cap lilies and harebells in April and May. Once you reach Balzer Herrgott, look out for the remains of a medieval Christian shrine — all that is visible now is the face of Christ, the rest of his figure having been enveloped in the trunk of a living tree. Follow the path that takes you into a deep ravine, known as the Wild Gutach, then cross the river and make your way to the Löwen Inn for lunch. The path then meanders upwards through dense woodland until you reach open pastures and the quaint village of St Märgen with its memorable twin-towered baroque church. The most comfortable place to stay is the Hirschen Hotel, where you can try local specialities including fresh wild trout, chanterelles and of course, the ubiquitous Black Forest gâteau.

Day 4: St Märgen to Titisee
22 km (14 miles), 6½ hours

Another early start; the path takes you on through the forest to Kalte Herberge which is said to be the watershed of Europe. Rain that falls on the western side flows down to the Rhine and eventually the North Sea; on the eastern side it joins the Danube and makes its way to the Black Sea. Continuing over the Hochberg Summit, 1,116 m (3,660 ft), you make your way to the small town of Titisee, which lies on the shores of a beautiful lake. Staying at the Treschers Schwarzwald-hotel, you will have unrivalled views over the water, as well as the use of the in-house spa which includes a sauna, swimming pool and massage treatments.

A TRADITIONAL BLACK FOREST FARMHOUSE

Day 5: Titisee to Bonndorf
22 km (13½ miles), 6 hours

Leaving the shores of Lake Titisee, you climb steeply but steadily to the Hochfirst Ridge at 1,200 m (4,000 ft). Although high, the views here are restricted by the density of the surrounding trees. However, from the top of a steel tower there is an excellent picture of the lake and the Feldberg. The staircase up is narrow and dark, so it is sensible to avoid it if you suffer from vertigo or claustrophobia. After wandering along the thickly wooded ridge, you pass through fields and on to the village of Kappel. On the way, you will see a number of traditional old farmhouses dating back to the 17th century. The space below their huge overhanging roofs was used to store hay for the cattle during the winter; this had the added benefit of providing much-needed insulation. After you have crossed the Haslach River it is worth stopping for lunch at the Löffelschmied Inn, which serves a range of outstanding local beers. Once you have climbed a wooded gorge and walked though the hamlet of Grönwald, follow the path signed to Bonndorf. The track is lined for much of the way with ferns, mosses and a thick layer of aromatic pine needles. The Gasthaus Zum Krantz, in the quiet town of Bonndorf, provides a comfortable resting place for the night.

Day 6: Bonndorf to Rötenbach
12 km (7½ miles), 4½ hours

Although this is the shortest day in walking terms, the scenery is spectacular. It is also the only time where you are unlikely to pass any inns during the middle part of the day (unless you get lost), so it is advisable to pack a picnic. Dropping down into the imposing Lothenbach Gorge, you will see a series of magnificent cataracts created by the turbulent Wutach River – which literally means 'fierce and angry'. After following the path along the Rötenbach Gorge, you will eventually come out at the small village of Rötenbach, where the Landgasthof Rossle Hotel is recommended. The village has several good bistros and you should have ample opportunity to try out some of the area's home-brewed liqueurs, such as the Kirschwasser (cherry), Mirabelle (golden plum) or Himbergeist (raspberry).

ALTERNATIVE ENTERTAINMENT ON LAKE TITISEE

Day 7: Rötenbach to Vöhrenbach
22 km (13½ miles), 6 hours

Several kilometres on from Rötenbach lies the village of Friedenweiler, with its picturesque monastery. Travelling through it, you make your way to Auf der Höchst, a modern factory town, and on to the picturesque village of Bubenbach. The walking is easy and in the summer you will pass lupins, broom and heather as you journey towards the village of Hammereisenbach, where the Hammer Inn serves the most delicious lunches. From here, you follow an old railway line through a narrow valley which leads to the 13th-century town of Vöhrenbach. Long associated with clock-making, the town also boasts a number of impressive half-timbered houses, one of which is the Gasthof Zum Ochsen. The oldest inn in the town, it provides a perfect setting for your final evening in the Black Forest.

Contact: World Walks
www.worldwalks.com
TEL: +44 (0) 1 242 254 353
FAX: +44 (0) 1 242 518 888

ONE OF THE MANY HAMLETS TUCKED AWAY IN THE HEART OF THE BLACK FOREST

In the far northwest of India lies the 'Land of Kings' — Rajasthan. The largest state in the country, it is renowned throughout the world for the magnificence of its palaces, forts, temples, mosques and tombs. This is the legacy of a rich history dominated by feudal warlords — the Rajputs. These warrior rulers first emerged in the 6th and 7th centuries; their behaviour was governed by rigid codes of chivalry, which resulted in endless internecine feuds. Despite this, they were honourable sovereigns and a popular belief at the time held that they were descended from the sun and the moon; even today they are still praised as gods by some communities.

- Route rating: easy
- 10 days/9 nights
- Dates: November to February

Rajasthan – Samode to Udaipur, India

Many of the Rajput's most savage battles were fought against the Muslim invaders who eventually, under the direction of the Mughal emperor Akbar, decided that cooperation and not subjugation was the only way forward. As a consequence, the fighting diminished after 1556, and resources that were generated from lucrative overland trading were showered on conspicuous displays of wealth — huge and luxurious palaces decorated throughout with intricate carpets, voluptuous silks, dazzling jewels and complex murals.

Despite its oases of grandeur, Rajasthan in the 21st century is one of the poorest states in India. Home to the Thar Desert, one of the driest places on earth, the region is frequently subject to drought and poverty is rife. However, southwest of the brown mountains of the Aravalli Range, the land becomes increasingly fertile and fields of wheat, maize, millet and cotton dominate the landscape. As you journey out to more remote areas, such as Sadar Samand, you see an outstanding array of birdlife including flamingos, pelicans, scarlet finches and iridescent kingfishers.

One of the main sources of income for the region is tourism, and many of the state's maharajas make ends meet financially by turning their family homes (usually a palace!) into what are known as 'heritage hotels'. These places are very comfortable and most have retained a unique charm. They also offer a sample some of the best cuisine in India, without exposing you to the dangers of food poisoning so common in most parts of the country.

This trip is a magical combination of walks through inspiring scenery and visits to superb cultural monuments. Winter (from November to February) is the best time of year to go, when the temperatures are low enough for you to need a jumper when you go outside. In summer, on the other hand, the temperatures can rise to 45°C (115°F) — unbearable!

**Day 1: Drive from Delhi to Samode,
6 hours; circular walk in Aravalli Hills
6 km (3½ miles), 2 hours**

Having flown into Delhi the night before,
you leave early in the morning to arrive
in the village of Samode, hidden in the
arid Aravalli Hills, in time to explore three
abandoned forts. To reach the first, the
Samode Fort, you have to climb up 300
steps, but the views across the rounded
hilltops more than justify the effort.
A stony path takes you past the next
two forts before leading you back to
the 18th-century Samode Palace, your
home for the next two nights. One of
the best palace hotels in India, it is
famous for its 300-year-old frescoes
and its mesmerizing Hall of Mirrors.

**Day 2: Drive to Amber, 1 hour; walk from
Amber to Jaipur 11 km (7 miles), 4 hours;
return to Samode**

By arriving early to explore the ancient
Amber Palace, home to the maharajas of
Jaipur, you will miss the hordes of tourists
guaranteed to arrive later in the day.
Following a zigzagging path, you arrive
at the massive Jaigarh Fort which houses
Asia's largest cannon. Ironically, this has
been a relatively peaceful area and the
cannon has never been fired in anger.
Jaipur can be seen in the distance as you
make your way to the Nahargarh Fort.
A further 6-km (4-mile) walk takes you
into the 'Pink City' itself — so called
because of the red colour-wash that is
used to stain the majority of the city's
buildings. Spend the afternoon exploring
Jaipur before returning by car to the
tranquillity of Samode.

**Day 3: Fly from Jaipur to Jodhpur;
drive to Luni, 45 minutes**

Luni is a tiny village south of Jodhpur
where the 19th-century Fort Chanwa,
with its temple and beautiful gardens,
makes an extraordinary place to stay.
Using this exceptionally good heritage
hotel as your base, you can explore the
surrounding hamlets and farms by jeep.

THE WOODEN TURRETS OF JAIGARH FORT OVERLOOKING JAIPUR

VIEW OVERLOOKING JAIPUR

Day 4: Luni to Rohetgarh
17 km (10½ miles), 5 hours

Walking through flat semi-desert, the homeland to the Bishnoi tribal community, you may see en route many different species of bird, including jungle babblers, rose-ringed parakeets and little green bee-eaters. Dromedary camels, water buffalo, sheep and goats populate the fields in the cultivated farmland. Lunch is taken at the 16th-century desert fort Rohetgarh — where Bruce Chatwin wrote his book *Songlines* and William Dalrymple started *City of Djins* — before a leisurely afternoon of free time.

Day 5: Drive from Rohetgarh to Sadar
Samand, 1.5 hours; walk round lake
6km (3½ miles), 1½ hours

Staying at the isolated Art Deco Sadar Samand Palace, on the top of a small hill overlooking a lake, you have the opportunity to see a spectacular array of water birds, such as egrets, brahminy duck, spoonbills and white ibis, to name but a few, either by walking round the lake or just watching from your balcony. At dinner, you are served an excellent selection of traditional Rajasthani dishes; the kedgeree, made with the beans from a local species of acacia tree, is a speciality.

Day 6: Drive to Khumbhalgarh Fort, 5 hours; circular walk, 4.8 km (3 miles)
The second most important fort in Rajasthan, Khumbhalgarh, lies in a heavily forested area of the Aravalli Hills. Dominating the pass from Ghanerao to Udaipur, it has 36 km (22½ miles) of walls, which in parts are thicker than the Great Wall of China. After exploring some of its 365 temples and shrines, make your way to the comfortable Aodhi Lodge in the centre of the adjacent Khumbhalgarh Wildlife Sanctuary.

Day 7: Aodhi Lodge to Ghanerao 17 km (10½ miles), 4½ hours
Following jeep tracks winding around the wildlife sanctuary, which provides a haven for wolves, leopards, panthers and marsh crocodiles among many others, you eventually arrive at the impossibly romantic but slightly run-down Ghanerao Royal Castle for lunch. The 50-km (30-mile) drive back to Aodhi takes 90 minutes.

THE INTRICATELY CARVED INTERIOR OF THE JAIN TEMPLE

Day 8: Aodhi Lodge to Ranakpur 15 km (9 miles), 4 hours
An undulating minor road heading west takes you to the site of a 15th-century Jain temple, noted for its spectacular architecture. Along the way you pass an extraordinary wealth of vegetation, including custard apples, bananas, mangoes, papaya and orange trees, all of which thrive in this fertile area. The temple, dedicated to Shiva-Mahadeva, is overrun with monkeys (black-faced langurs), but is blissfully free of tourists. To enter it you must not wear shoes, shorts, vests or anything made of leather. Only 4 km (2½ miles) away lies the Maharani Bagh Orchard Retreat, set among a series of mango orchards, which provides a peaceful and comfortable place to stay.

Day 9: Drive to Udaipur 3 hours; walk to Monsoon Palace 6 km (3½ miles), 3 hours
Described as one of the most romantic cities in India, Udaipur is graced with elegant white palaces, deep blue lakes and emerald-green hills. Leaving the five-star Shiv Niwas Palace Hotel (where you spend the night), with its panoramic views over Lake Pichola, you make your way to the 19th-century Monsoon Palace. Very few people visit this palace, despite its unrivalled views over Udaipur – primarily because you have to make a special request to be allowed to enter it. However, the hassle is worthwhile – witnessing the 360-degree panorama at sunset is a sight never to be forgotton.

Day 10: Return to Delhi

THE SPECTACULAR JAIN TEMPLE SURROUNDED BY DENSE FOREST

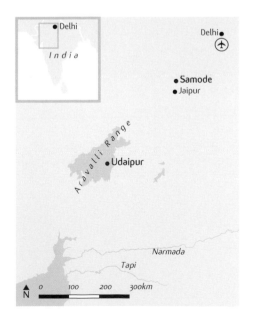

Contact: ATG Oxford

www.atg-oxford.co.uk

TEL: +44 (0)1 865 315 678

FAX: +44 (0)1 865 315 697

Himachal Pradesh in northern India, sandwiched between Tibet and the Punjab, has an extraordinarily diverse landscape. Subtropical forests, orchards, rice paddies and cornfields flourish in its fertile valleys, while ice-fields and snow cling to the perilous peaks of its mountain ranges which soar to over 6,000 m (19,200 ft).

- Route rating: moderate—fairly strenuous
- 11 days/10 nights
- Dates: from October to April

Abode of the Gods – Pathankot to Dharamkot, India

While being a popular destination for trekkers, much of the region remains totally unspoilt and the daily living of local mountain tribal peoples continues in the same patterns that have existed for hundreds of years. Travelling to Dharamakot, at the foot of the Dhauladhar Mountains in the north of the province, you have the opportunity to walk in some of the most remote areas of India. Using the paths of the Gaddi shepherds, who live a semi-nomadic lifestyle following an age-old cycle as they move their flocks from one grazing pasture to the next, you travel in a circuit through a wildlife sanctuary packed to the gunnels with flora and fauna. Black bears, porcupines and leopards are common, along with langur and rhesus monkeys, jackals and — in the mountains — the local equivalent of the yeti, known as a gye.

Flying up to 5,000 m (16,000 ft), golden eagles and griffons hunt the skies for food, while in the forests below woodpeckers, rose finches and Himalayan bulbuls flit from branch to branch; closer to the hill stations of Dharamsala and McLeod-Ganj you will see scarlet minivets and yellow-breasted greenfinches. For those who are passionate about butterflies, more than 112 species have been identified along this particular walk.

In order to travel safely and to discover the maximum about your surroundings, historically, geographically and botanically, a local guide is indispensable. One of the best is Mark Butterworth, an Englishman who grew up in India and who speaks Hindustani and Pahari (Gaddi dialect). His close relations with the Gaddi mean that he can visit areas inaccessible to most Europeans. Because of the remote region, you spend most nights in tents which, along with your luggage and the rest of the equipment, are carried by porters.

Reaching a maximum altitude of 4,075 m (13,040 ft), you need to pack some warm clothes because, despite the fact that temperatures can rise to 20–25°C (68–77°F) in the valleys, it cools down very quickly as soon as you start to climb. At the higher levels, there is a chance that you will fall prey to altitude sickness unless you drinks lots of water and take time to acclimatize. Warning signs include loss of appetite, headaches, nausea and tiredness; slowly moving back downhill should alleviate minor symptoms. The best way to avoid these problems is to introduce yourself slowly to the altitude and use the time to soak up the etheral atmosphere and outstanding vistas.

THE BASPA RIVER IN HIMACHAL PRADESH

THE DHAULADHAR MOUNTAINS

Day 1: Overnight train from Delhi to Pathankot; drive to McLeod-Ganj, 2½ hours

Towered over by the severe rock faces of the Dhauladhar Mountains, the picturesque 'double town' of McLeod-Ganj and its lower part, Dharamsala, is spread over several wooded ridges. Once a British hill station, the combined town is now the home of the Dalai Lama and the Tibetan Government in exile. There is time for you to explore the narrow streets, museum and Buddhist temples before returning to the delightful Chonor House Hotel (where all profits go to preserving Tibetan culture).

Day 2: McLeod-Ganj to Gehra
11 km (7 miles), 5 hours

Climbing through a pine and rhododendron forest you reach the highest point of the day's walk, 2,042 m (6,700 ft), before descending slightly to the Dal Lake for an early lunch. Continuing along a bridle-track past several hamlets, you arrive at Gehra, 1,829 m (5,990 ft), with its small bazaar and secluded riverside campsite.

Day 3: Gehra to Noli
10.4 km (6½ miles), 5 hours
A steady ascent up winding shepherd's trails takes you through a lush valley to the village of Kerai, which spreads out over the hillside for several kilometres. Along the way you may see villagers spinning and weaving wool from the precious herds of sheep and goats. Fields dotted with water buffalo give way to an oak and spruce forest as the trail brings you to Noli, the gateway to the domain of the Gaddi shepherds, and your campsite by the old wooden bridge.

Day 4: Noli to Belani River
11.4 km (7 miles), 6 hours
Be prepared to be woken early with your morning cup of tea today in order to strike camp by 8.30. Continuing up the valley towards the Dhauladhar Mountains, you follow the path of the Belani River through more rhododendron forest and past Gaddi encampments. A peaceful campsite near the river will be where you set up camp for this evening. There are some enticing aquamarine pools you can swim in, although this is not for the faint-hearted as they are extremely cold.

Day 5: Belani River to Kereri Lake
4.8 km (3 miles), 3 hours
It is a long, tiring climb, 750 m (2,500 ft) up a steep ridge through a thick pine and oak forest to the shores of Kereri Lake at the base of the Minkianni Pass 3,200 m (10,500 ft). Once there, however, you will be treated to the sight of some beautiful meadows which in spring are awash with wildflowers including potentillas, saxifrage and gentians. While camp is being set up in sheltered spot by the lake, you can visit the small temple that stands on the bank. If you have the energy to climb the surrounding high ridges, you will be rewarded with spectacular views of the Kangra Valley below.

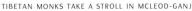
TIBETAN MONKS TAKE A STROLL IN MCLEOD-GANJ

Day 6: Kereri Lake to Rhella
12 km (7½ miles), 5 hours

After a leisurely breakfast of chapattis, rhododendron leaf jam (a local speciality) and *chai* (tea), you have a relaxed walk down through pristine valleys filled with wild chestnut trees, meadows and clear mountain streams. Don't be tempted to drink the water from these streams without treating it with iodine or some other purification system first. The campsite at Rhella stands at 2,438 m (8,000 ft).

Day 7: Rhella to a forest glade
1.4 km (7 miles), 5 hours

Gaddi paths take you into a remote hinterland and up to a high plateau with marvellous views of the Dhauladhar Mountains. As you pass the tiny, intermittent hamlets you will find the local people curious about you, especially the children who stare at you with huge, wondering eyes; unlike many parts of Asia, however, here the children never beg. In the afternoon, you descend through thick woodland before coming to a tranquil forest glade — so far from anywhere that it doesn't even have a name.

A TRADITIONAL RICE FIELD

Day 8: Forest glade to Laka River
13.6 km (8½ miles), 6 hours

This is one of the most demanding day's walking. Continuing through the forest and out on to undulating ridges, you then descend towards Guna Temple, 2,134 m (7,000 ft), a sacred pilgrimage centre for the Gaddi shepherds. From here you have a gentle afternoon walk to the banks of the Laka River and your campsite, at a mere 1,981 m (6,500 ft).

Day 9: Laka River to Triund
12 km (7½ miles), 5 hours

Looking down to the terraced fields and herds of sheep and goats grazing in a cultivated valley, you reach the Gullu Ridge. Following the line of the ridge, you climb to 450 m (1,500 ft) until you arrive at Triund, situated on a broad open plateau at the foot of the Dhauladhar Mountains. From your campsite in a meadow you can see right across the Beas Dam to the Indian plains beyond.

Day 10: Triund to Dharamkot
11.4 km (7 miles), 4 hours;
drive to McLeod-Ganj

Walking along a ridge behind the prayer flags and above the Gaddi encampment, you have a gentle climb through spruce and oak forests up to Laka Got, 3,350 m (10,900 ft), situated at the foot of the Indrahar Pass. With a series of jagged snow-capped peaks above, you make your way along the Laka Ridge and then down, through the wildlife sanctuary, to your final destination of Dharamkot. The views in the distance of the nearby Kangra Valley are excellent, and in the surrounding foliage you will hear the gentle calls of Chir and Khalij pheasants. Your final evening in the area is spent at the comfortable Chonor House Hotel whose restaurant provides some of the very best vegetarian Tibetan food in the town.

Day 11: Return to Delhi

Contact: Sherpa Expeditions
www.sherpaexpeditions.com
TEL: +44 (0)20 8577 2717
FAX: +44 (0)20 8572 9788

The soaring peaks of the Brenta Dolomites, which form part of the Italian Alps, were once a coral reef. During the Triassic period, over 200 million years ago, the area was covered by a tropical sea, which dispersed as the Alps began to form. Now, the Dolomites reach heights of between 2,000 and 3,000 m (6,560 and 9,340 ft), but as you climb the paths towards their glacier-serrated crags, you may well find small marine fossils in the scree at your feet. When the sun sets on the mountains, the rock turns pink — a phenomenon known as 'alpenglow' — and the views are magnificent.

- Route rating: fairly strenuous
- 8 days/7 nights
- Dates: July to September

Brenta Dolomites – Madonna di Campiglio to Molveno, Italy

The Brenta Range, which lies north-west of the region's principal city of Trento and is relatively close to the border with Austria, forms the backbone of the Parco Naturale Adamello-Brenta — Trentino's largest protected area. Over 82 species of bird live in the park, including ptarmigan and eagles, and there is plenty of other wildlife to look out for, from chamois to marmots and the odd brown bear. The landscape varies from alpine meadowland through to forests, which slowly give way to a jagged and barren moonscape. One of the most interesting aspects of the local topography is the number of hanging glaciers, which never move and form essentially permanent swathes of ice, found in particular on steep mountain sides.

This expedition traverses the Brenta Dolomites by way of an exceptionally exhilarating route. At times the walking is very steep and the drops can be sheer, so if you suffer from vertigo then you may find some aspects of the trip difficult. Although the paths are well maintained, it is a good idea to bring at least one walking stick with you. Three of the nights are spent in mountain refuges, high up among the peaks. The accommodation, even though it includes ready-made beds, is basic, and you will need to carry your own luggage (a change of warm clothes, washing things and waterproofs) to these huts. However, the atmosphere in the refuges is extremely welcoming and each has a bar and restaurant.

You need to be pretty fit to complete the trip — the ascent to the first refuge takes three hours and spans 713 m (2,379 ft). The effort is more than rewarded by the isolated splendour of your surroundings when you reach the top. Temperatures can rise to 27°c (80°F) or more, although at higher altitudes there is usually snow all year round and the temperatures tend to drop. The weather ought to be good, but as with all mountainous regions it can change at a moment's notice. The best months to visit are July and early September; it is wise to avoid the first three weeks of August because the mountains are relatively crowded then, and there is often a heat haze that rises from the valleys and obscures the views.

Day 1: Madonna di Campiglio

After a three-and-a-half hour drive from Verona airport you arrive at the small mountain resort of Madonna di Campiglio. This resort stands on the site of a mountain hospice dating back more than 800 years, and was a favourite haunt of the Austrian emperor Franz Joseph in the 19th century. Other than being home to the oldest golf course in Italy, it is popular today as a centre for walking and skiing. One of the best places to stay is the four-star Chalet Hermitage, which stands in a private park and boasts impressive spa facilities. Here you will also have every opportunity to sample some of the area's finest delicacies, including caraway-scented breads, *polenta e coniglio* (polenta with game) and *strangolapreti* (spinach gnocci).

VIEW OF THE BRENTA DOLOMITES FROM MADONNA DI CAMPIGLIO

Day 2: Circular walk above Lake Malghette
**8 km (5 miles), 30 minute drive,
3 hours walking**

This is a pleasant and not unduly strenuous walk with which to start the trip, although there are one or two steep moments in the afternoon. After a short car journey to the Carlo Magno Pass, you make your way up through thick evergreen forests until you reach the Rifugio Malghette beside which stands a secluded lake. This makes a perfect spot for lunch, and you rarely find any other people here. Continuing upwards you come across two more lakes – Alto and Scuro – both wild and untouched. Alpenrose blossom near the water's edge and the higher slopes are covered with potentilla and gentian. The circular route takes you back to Lake Malghette, from where you head down to the Hermitage.

Day 3: Madonna di Campiglio to Rifugio Tuckett 9.3 km (5½ miles), 4 hours

The delightful start to this walk follows a meandering path beside a trickling stream, and up through shady woods of beech and pine. Red and yellow waymarks direct you past gushing waterfalls, along a zigzagging path that eventually emerges into open meadowland at the top. Here you should be able to find more alpenroses and various orchids, including nigritella and lady's slipper. Shortly after this, by continuing along the path, you will arrive at Rifugio Casinei, 1,829 m (5,990 ft), which if you are feeling a bit wobbly is a sensible stop-off point for lunch. From here you continue the gradual ascent until you reach the eyrie-like Rifugio Tuckett, 2,272 m (7,498 ft), with its outstanding views of Mount Castelletto Inferiore.

Day 4: Rifugio Tuckett to Rifugio Alimonta
8 km (5 miles); 4 hours

The trickiest part of today's walk is negotiating the slippery limestone pavement at the foot of the descent from Tuckett. Once this is out of the way, you drop briefly back down below the tree line before heading up past the Rifugio Brentei. Little clumps of edelweiss line the path, which grows increasingly steep and rocky: at one stage there is a steel rope to help you complete the most difficult section. The Rifugio Alimonta lies just ahead of this; at 2,539 m (8,464 ft) it is the high point, literally, of your journey.

Day 5: Rifugio Alimonta to Rifugio Pedrotti
5.6 km (3½ miles), 4 hours

The steep descent back down to Brentei appears fairly hair-raising, but it looks worse than it is. However, you will need to gather all your stamina for the trek over the pass at Bocca di Brenta, 2,552 m (8,422 ft) and it's a good idea to have some chocolate before you start the 90-minute ascent. Also, put some extra layers on, as there is invariably snow lying on the ground and the temperature drops noticeably. The terrain is precipitous, rocky and often icy; in places there is a rope to help you and, at these points it is essential to ditch the walking sticks and use both hands. Scary as it is, it is impossible not to be dumbfounded by the sheer majesty of your surroundings. Once you reach the pass, it is only a 15-minute walk down to the Rifugio Pedrotti, where you will be assured of a warm welcome and some hearty food, including home-made vegetable soup, pasta and delicious local cheeses.

Day 6: Rifugio Pedrotti to Molveno
10.8 km (6½ miles); 5 hours

From the craggy wilderness of the Brenta peaks, you descend over 1,607 m (5,356 ft) to the town of Molveno. It is fascinating to see how the flora and fauna change once you reach the tree line. Now and again you may see marmots; slowly wildflowers, such as the rare lilac-coloured devil's-claw, reappear. There are a few steep, slippery sections as you pass through a mixed-wood forest but they are nothing compared to what you have already walked over. The path to Molveno is clearly marked and, as you journey lower, it is carpeted with cyclamens, as well as purple and yellow cow-wheat flowers. If you are lucky you may see some red-headed grouse or a capercaillie. Eventually – and somewhat prosaically – you reach a car park. From here it is a short walk to the Grand Hotel, with its beautiful lakeside garden and pool. After the simplicity of the refuges, it is an oasis of luxury.

Day 7: Day in Molveno
Optional 3½ hour walk round lake

After the rigours of the previous few days, it is a treat to sit back and soak in the beauty of this charming town. If you are feeling energetic you can do a three-and-a-half-hour circuit of the lake which includes a Roman bridge and Napoleon's Fort, as well as a pretty waterfall. Alternatively, you can venture into the town centre and visit the 12th-century church, which is painted with frescoes both inside and out. There are numerous cafés and restaurants, but the Antica Bosnia is notable because it is situated in one of the few remaining medieval buildings. After a relaxed evening back at the Grand Hotel, you will feel refreshed for your journey home.

Day 8: Return to Verona by car.

COWS GRAZING ON THE HILLSIDES IN TRENTINO

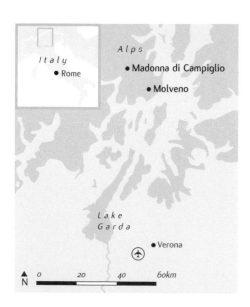

Contact: ATG Oxford

www.atg-oxford.co.uk

TEL: +44 (0)1 865 315 678

FAX: +44 (0)1 865 315 697

Umbria, the 'green heart of Italy', surely has to be one of the world's most beautiful battlefields. As well as being one of the few landlocked regions of Italy, it is also exceptionally fertile, and was fought over incessantly from the Dark Ages to the 16th century. Sandwiched between its two more famous neighbours, Lazio and Tuscany, Umbria is to a large degree ignored by the many tourists who pop in to visit its most celebrated asset, Assisi, before rushing off to pound the streets of Rome or Florence.

Umbria — Todi to Assisi, Italy

- Route rating: moderate
- 8 days/7 nights
- Dates: from late April to December

Umbria's rolling hills are home to many unspoilt medieval towns and hamlets, however, rich with art and architecture (ranging from Etruscan and Roman to Romanesque and Renaissance). Despite this and its undoubted scenic splendour, the further you travel into the countryside the more likely you are to find it completely free of other visitors. The local people are exceptionally warm and friendly, and will chat happily with you over a *grappa* or a coffee for hours on end.

As well as offering a visual feast, Umbria is renowned for its simple but exquisite food. Most dishes contain no more than three or four ingredients, but the combination of flavours is sublime: fresh black truffles, cold-pressed olive oil, wood-scented porcini. The golden wines from Orvieto and distinctive reds from Montefalco are among the finest in Italy, although in more rural parts of Umbria you will be offered equally delicious local wines.

'The Way to Assisi' follows age-old paths between some of the area's finest medieval towns, starting in the ancient walled city of Todi and ending in the magnificent metropolis of Assisi. Many of these places were damaged by the violent earthquakes of 1997, which saw the collapse of the Basilica di San Francesco in Assisi. Renovations have been completed and almost all the monuments have reopened. The walking itself is fairly leisurely, with plenty of time to stop off and sightsee en route. However, there are a few steep descents and ascents, particularly on the last day when you climb over Mount Subasio, 1,269 m (4,162 ft). The best months to visit are April and May, when all the wildflowers are blooming, although September and October are equally stunning and pleasantly warm. It is wise to avoid the area in July and August, however, when temperatures are high and the tourists are out in force.

VIEW OF ASSISI

Day 1: Drive from Rome to Todi, 2½ hours

The journey from Rome grows increasingly scenic as you wind your way up into the verdant Umbrian hills. The landscape is dominated by fields of sunflowers, lush green forests and geometrically ordered olive groves. Todi is beautifully situated on the top of a craggy hill and its origins are said to date back to 2700BC. Before you enter the medieval walls surrounding the old part of the city, stop off and visit the delightful Renaissance church of Santa Maria della Consolazione. Walking up through the winding little streets of Todi to the historic centre you find the Hotel Fonte Cesia, housed in a 13th-century palazzo. Its comfortable interior is decorated with 19th-century antiques and dark wood panelling.

Day 2: Todi to Bevagna
18.7 km (11½ miles), 5½ hours

From Todi you can see on the horizon the Monti Martani, a range of hills rising to 914 m (3,000 ft); they are your destination for today. It is best to leave relatively soon after breakfast as the morning's walk is mainly uphill. Passing through open farmland it offers panoramic views but little shade, so remember to wear a broad-brimmed sunhat and to take lots of water. As you reach the woodland areas the walking becomes much more gentle, allowing you to get your breath back before starting the climb over the Monti Martani. The views at the top are marvellous, and from mid-May to mid-June the flowers, including scabious, rock roses, narcissi and orchids, are breathtaking. The gravel underfoot makes the descent from the hills particularly tiring. However, once you reach Giano dell'Umbria, it is only a short drive to Bevagna, where the Orto degli Angeli provides an elegant place to stay in the centre of this medieval village.

Day 3: Giano dell'Umbria circuit via Montefalco 20.4 km (12½ miles); 6 hours

It's worth taking a little time out to explore some of Giano dell'Umbria's churches and frescos, which date back to the 15th century, before heading out over farmland to another walled medieval town, Montefalco. Passing olive groves, vineyards and small farming hamlets, you will see a landscape that has remained remarkably constant for hundreds of years. The walking is gentle until the final climb into Montefalco, which sits at the end of a ridge running towards Bevagna. It offers fantastic 360-degree views over the entire Spoleto vale, which are even better when seen from the top of the Palazzo del Comune's tower. After this, make your way back down to Bevagna for a second night at the Orto degli Angeli.

Day 4: Bevagna to Spello
10.8 km (6½ miles), 3½ hours

After spending the morning exploring the two 12th-century Romanesque churches (bring some binoculars with you so you can really appreciate the extraordinary detail in the façades) as well as the medieval paper factory, you set off across an agricultural plain for the Roman town of Spello. The walking is over very flat ground which in hot weather is renowned for causing blisters, so make sure you wear well-fitting footwear. One of the best hotels to stay in is the grand Palazzo Bocci.

OLIVE GROVES OUTSIDE SPELLO

Day 5: Free day in Spello

Known as Hispellum in Roman times, Spello still retains some of it 1st century Augustan walls, and just outside the town are the ruins of a Roman amphitheatre. With its cobbled streets and hanging houses (archways above the streets connecting one building to another), it exudes a bewitching medieval charm. It is also renowned for its outstanding frescos, the best of which is the Cappella Baglioni in the church of Santa Maria Maggiore. Painted by Pinturicchio (which literally means 'the Rich Painter'!) in 1501, this depicts the birth of Christ. Equally impressive monuments worth seeing include the Porta Consolare (the original pre-Augustan Roman gateway), the Pinacoteca Comunale, which houses a collection of medieval art, and the church of Sant'Andrea. There are numerous taverns where you can sit and watch the world go by — very slowly — while you sample some of the area's delicacies, such as smoked wood-flavoured pasta with mushrooms and truffles.

Day 6: Spello to Assisi
17.7 km (11 miles); 5 hours

Leaving the Roman forum in Spello, you follow gravel tracks through olive groves and scrub, moving on to woodland paths as you make your way up Mount Subasio, 1,269 m (4,162 ft), until you reach an area of meadowland. The views and the wildflowers are equally dazzling, and if the weather is good you can wander right along the top of the mountain until you begin to descend into the woods towards Assisi. The temperature at the top is substantially lower than in the valleys, so bring something warm and waterproof. The last hour of the walk is over fairly rough ground, but the approach to Assisi, on the pilgrim's path from the Hermitage, is superb. Walking down through the old town you come to the award-winning Hotel Fontebella. Its restaurant, Il Frantoio, is one of the best in the city.

Day 7: Cultural walk round Assisi
9.6 km (6 miles), 6 hours

Sitting on a foothill of Mount Subasio, Assisi has been a place of pilgrimage for nearly a thousand years. It is bursting with fascinating art and architecture and, starting your day in the Piazza del Comune, you will see the Tempio di Minerva, which is said to have one of the most perfect Roman façades in the country. From here you can move on to the beautiful frescos in the 15th-century Oratorio dei Pellegrini, before arriving at the famous Basilica di San Francesco. From the Basilica di Santa Chiara it is a short walk out of Assisi to the small church of San Damiano, which remains much the same as it was when St Francis was alive in the early 1200s. After a visit to the Cattedrale San Rufino, the final stop on your tour ought to be the Rocca Maggiore, the city's intriguing medieval fortress.

Day 8: Return to Rome by car

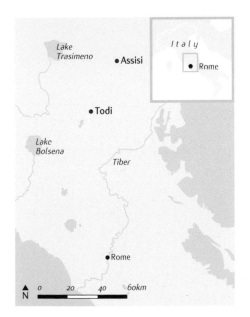

Contact: ATG Oxford
www.atg-oxford.co.uk
TEL: +44 (0)1 865 315 678
FAX: +44 (0)1 865 315 697

The Kerry Way
– Killarney to Caherciveen, Ireland

From before the Roman era, throughout medieval times and up until relatively recently, pilgrimage was often nothing more than a thinly veiled excuse for rampant tourism. In times when travelling for the sake of enjoyment alone was not a justifiable option, you had to be seen to have a proper reason for touring, and the word 'pilgrimage' became an effective cover-all. However, there are some parts of the world which are just so beautiful, so spiritual and so fundamentally addictive that it has been generally accepted for years that when you go to visit them, you go for no other reason than purely to soak up the atmosphere.

• Route rating: easy–moderate
• 8 days/7 nights
• Dates: all year round

The Iveragh Peninsula in southwest Ireland is one such place. Since the 1700s people have flocked to the area, drawn by its dramatic scenery and the legendary conviviality of its population. The peninsula has an ancient history of civilization. The remains of Bronze Age forts litter the countryside, the most notable being Staigue Fort, near Caherdaniel, which has walls that are 5.5 m (18 ft) high and 4 m (13 ft) thick. The landscape is extremely varied – in Killarney National Park the vegetation is lush; the rugged wilderness of mid-Kerry is home to deep peat bogs and Ireland's highest mountain, Carrauntuohill, 1,041 m (3,414 ft). And the path from Glenbeigh to Foilmore is one of the most scenic coastal routes in Europe.

PEAT CUTTING NEAR GLENBEIGH

The area's moors and boglands provide a home for hares, foxes and Ireland's only herd of native red deer. From the skies the poignant song of skylarks and meadow pipits accompanies you for much of your journey, while the harsher whistles of the curlew grow frequent as you head towards the coast. In late summer, you ought to be able to see the pink flowers of cross-leaved heath, along with bilberries, cowberries and greater butterwort.

Kerry benefits from the warm currents of the Gulf Stream and has a mild and moist climate, with an average temperature of about 7°C (45°F) in mid-winter and 16°C (61°F) in mid-summer. There are up to 18 hours of daylight in summer, and the only downside is the area's high rainfall. Even this is not much of a problem as long as you take waterproof clothes and assume that, at some stage each day, you are probably going to get wet. The rain brings with it other benefits – approaching storm clouds create dramatic scenes over the mountain summits and often you will see two or three rainbows at the same time.

The Kerry Way follows old drovers' and trading tracks for much of the time; the full route takes some eleven days and covers 196 km (122 miles). This version, however, is shorter and fits comfortably into seven days. As with all things in Kerry, it is taken at a leisurely pace, with plenty of opportunities to stop for a pint of Guinness.

Day 1: Killarney (30 minute drive from the airport)

After flying into Kerry airport you ought to have enough time to wander around the attractive town of Killarney, or Cill Arne as it is known in Gaelic, meaning Church of the Sloes. There was a church foundation here as early as the 6th century, and today the town's Christian heritage is still very strong; St Mary's Cathedral is an impressive building worth visiting for its original 1870s organ. The town depends on tourism for its survival, and there is a broad range of places where you can stay — one of the best is the Killarney Park Hotel, which is also conveniently close to Killarney Golf Course.

VIEW OF ROSS CASTLE NEAR KILLARNEY

Day 2: Killarney to Black Valley
20.8 km (13 miles), 6 hours

Queen Victoria described Killarney and its surrounding countryside as a 'fairyland'. With its unspoilt forests, stunning lakes and mountainous backdrops, it's not hard to understand why. One of the first natural wonders you see at the start of this walk is Torc Waterfall, a 12-m (40-ft) cascading delight surrounded by leafy green deciduous trees. Crossing a stone bridge above it, you walk along a minor road, with Mangerton Mountain on one side of you and Torc Mountain on the other. Leaving the rhododendron-bedecked Owengarriff River behind you, you cross a rocky ravine and enter a natural oak forest beside the Upper Lake of Killarney, home to red squirrels who scamper quickly from tree to tree as you approach. The landscape grows more barren as you make your way into the Black Valley and your lodgings at Hillcrest Farmhouse. There are very few places to stay in this area, so it is important to book well in advance.

Day 3: Black Valley to Glencar
20.8 km (13 miles), 7 hours

Under the shadow of Macgillycuddy's Reeks with the massive red sandstone mountains to the east, you make your way along a bridle path across the brooding wilderness of the Black Valley, passing the ruins of an abandoned hamlet. Once you have climbed over a ridge into the Bridia Valley, the track zigzags up to a pass at 350 m (1,120 ft) which lies between Curraghmore, 850 m (2,822 ft), and an unnamed peak. On a clear day, you can see for many kilometres and can appreciate the majesty of these imposing glens carved out by the passage of glaciers thousands of years ago. Meeting the tarmac road west of Lough Acoose, it is a 3 km (2 mile) walk to Glencar, where the Glencar House Hotel has wonderful views of the mountains and an exceptionally well stocked bar.

Day 4: Glencar to Glenbeigh
17 km (11 miles), 5 hours

The route from Glencar provides magical views over Caragh Lake, and is much gentler than yesterday's walk. Crossing the Caragh River, you follow forestry tracks until you reach Blackstone Bridge and then begin the climb over the shoulder of one of the Seefin Mountains. From here there is a good track down to Glenbeigh and the welcoming warmth of the Towers Hotel, which has the added attraction of an effective clothes-drying room.

THE ATMOSPHERIC TORC WATERFALL

Day 5: Glenbeigh – optional half-day circular walks

Glenbeigh is a small fishing and holiday village nestling in the foot of the Seefin Mountains, with a 6.4-km (4-mile) pristine beach to explore. The views across Dingle Bay to the Dingle Mountains are world famous, and if the water is warm enough (or rather if your constitution is strong enough) there are great opportunities for swimming. For the adventurous, horseriding, canoeing, windsurfing and hang-gliding are on offer. If you are visiting at the end of the summer, try to ensure that your trip coincides with the annual village festival in August, which includes two days of horse racing on the beach. There are a number of half-day circular walks from which you can choose all taking you up into the Seefins, where you will discover a series of glacial corries and lakes.

Day 6: Glenbeigh to Foilmore
18 km (11 miles), 5½ hours

Walking out of Glenbeigh you make your way to Glenbeigh woods, where you climb through heather and ferns until you reach a point where you can look down on Behy Valley and over to Rossbehy Peninsula. Continuing upwards, you skirt the shoulder of Drung Hill. From here you will be able to survey the best possible views of Dingle Bay and the vast Atlantic Ocean. The path follows an early Christian route, and it is a strange feeling to realize that much of what you see has changed little from what the pilgrims saw hundreds of years ago. Heading down through a forestry plantation you make your way to Fransal House, a comfortable B&B with an extremely relaxed and friendly atmosphere.

Day 7: Foilmore to Caherciveen
9.6 km (6 miles), 3 hours

It's a relaxed morning of gentle walking as you follow the route over bogland, past a series of farms, towards the capital of the Iveragh Peninsula, Caherciveen. Along the way you see a number of peat hags, where small rectangles of turf are cut out and left in triangular piles to dry out before being used as winter fuel. Caherciveen is a charming place — situated at the foot of Benetee Mountain, it has breathtaking views, and each year painters from around the world journey to the town to produce their own interpretations of the truly extraordinary landscapes around it.

After spending the afternoon exploring the town's architectural and archaeological sites, including Ballycarbery Castle (a 15th-century tower house) and Leacanabuille and Caherine stone forts — both of which are impressive examples of dry stone masonry dating back to 800/900AD — you will be more than ready to head to the Caherciveen Park Hotel for some well-eaned rest and recuperation.

Day 8: Drive to Kerry Airport, 1 hour

Contact: Sherpa Expeditions
www.sherpaexpeditions.com
TEL: +44 (0)20 8577 2717
FAX: +44 (0)20 8572 9788

'Savage and backward' is how the Chinese referred to the inhabitants of Japan in 200BC. Yet by 400AD, Japanese society had changed beyond all recognition, and Chinese culture and technology were being imported wholesale into the country. So effective was this rapid development that the centralized state originally organized by the ancestors of the present Japanese royal family still forms the basis for today's bastions of power – Tokyo, Kyoto and Osaka. However, the creation of new cities and the administrative systems required to run them meant a network of roads was needed to ensure that taxes could be collected and the provinces controlled effectively.

- Route rating: easy–moderate
- 10 days/9 nights
- Dates: March to June

Nakasendo Way – Kyoto to Narai, Japan

The origins of the Nakasendo Highway, which spanned from Kyoto to Tokyo, date back to the 7th century. It was a typical product of the imperial Chinese pattern of road building – lined with trees, well maintained and regularly interspersed with carefully ordered post-towns, where inns, and shops catered to the traveller's needs. There were strict rules as to who was allowed to journey along it – only the governing classes, foreign diplomats and, latterly, merchants. The only way anyone else was permitted to use the highway was to claim to be a pilgrim. Even then, many of the lower classes could not afford to travel, so whole villages would club together to send one or two members of their community off on a pilgrimage, and then wait with high anticipation for the exotic stories that would be told on their return.

In modern Japan, much of the original Nakasendo Highway has been lost to urban sprawl, which is anything but walking-friendly. Telephone poles, gaping drainage ditches and uneven surfaces characterize the sidewalks, and most Japanese prefer to cycle or use the train rather than go on foot. However, parts of the Nakasendo Highway remain utterly unspoilt, and offer walkers a privileged insight into quiet areas of the country that most visitors miss completely. Passing through hills and farmland, you stay in traditional inns along the route where Europeans are virtually unseen. The countryside is remarkably varied, and the only downside is that to avoid the more built-up areas, regular train-trips are needed to take you to and from the rural communities.

This walk, best undertaken from March to June when the temperatures are mild (although you will still need to bring a waterproof jacket with you), only takes you along the most beautiful parts of the highway. As you stay in many places off the beaten track, it is important to learn a bit about Japanese etiquette. You won't be expected to get everything right, but just by trying you will endear yourself to your hosts, who invariably display a kindness and generosity that is humbling.

KISHOJI TEMPLE

Day 1: Arrival in Kyoto

After arriving at Kansai International Airport, it's an hour's train journey to Kyoto, where you can get a taste of things to come by spending your first night in a traditional Japanese inn or *ryokan*. Slippers will be placed in the front porch for you to change into on arrival, and your bedding is hidden behind sliding doors: you lay it out and make it up each night. One of the best *ryokans* in the city centre is the Yoshikawa, which is renowned for its *tempura kaiseki* cuisine.

Day 2: Kyoto

Northwest Kyoto is home to some of the city's most famous temples, gardens and shrines. The Temple of the Golden Pavilion, with its beautiful lake-garden, is a good place to start. The austere 15th-century Zen garden at Ryoanji is equally impressive but often crowded, and you would do just as well to visit the eminently peaceful temple and moss garden of Saihoji. Moving back to central Kyoto, you can look forward to good traditional cooking for dinner at the local restaurant Fujinoya.

THE TEMPLE OF THE GOLDEN PAVILLION IN KYOTO

Day 3: Train to Hikone; walk around Hikone, 11.4 km (7 miles), 4½ hours; train to Sekigahara

A short train ride takes you to Hikone, a classic example of a medieval feudal castle town. Walking through the former geisha quarter and the bustling merchant district, you come to the town's impressive castle with its myriad pointed roofs. From this magical setting you take the train to Sekigahara, site of a decisive battle in 1600 which ended a century of civil war. Spending the night at a *ryokan*, you are likely to be served a delicious hot-pot of beef stewed in soy, sugar and *sake* broth.

Day 4: Train to Mitake; walk to Hosokute, 12 km (7½ miles), 4 hours

Travelling through the Mino Plain, past Nagoya, and into the foothills beyond, you arrive at one of the very first post-towns to be developed on the Nakasendo Highway — Mitake. Walking along the route, through paddy fields and wooded hills, you readily find evidence of the old highway; shrines for the foot-weary and lines of trees under which to rest. Arriving at the remote post-town of Hosokute at sundown, you will see a lantern hanging outside the highway's only remaining 17th-century inn, Daikokuya, where you can expect to eat freshwater fish and mountain vegetable dishes.

Day 5: Mitake to Ena 22 km (14 miles), 5½ hours

A country road lined with pines, which once used to stretch the whole length of the Nakasendo Highway, takes you past manicured rice paddies, lotus ponds and farmsteads up to the Biwa Pass, where a stone inscription records a heartbreaking poem written by a 19th-century princess forced to marry against her wishes. From here it is a gentle walk down to Okute, with its 1,200-year-old cedar tree standing in the grounds of a shrine, for lunch. The route in the afternoon follows a 7th-century footpath along the top of a ridge, known as the Thirteen Passes, which takes you down to the city of Ena.

Day 6: Ena to Shinchaya
19.3 km (12 miles); 5 hours

After stopping off at an ancient Zen temple on the outskirts of Ena, you walk on through farmland to a rolling valley which leads you to the former post-town of Nakatsugawa. Once you have stopped for lunch here, the long walk (2 to 3 hours) to Shinchaya begins. The majority of the way is uphill, but the views over the hilly countryside are impressive and the last part of the journey passes over the best-kept and most photogenic section of the highway. An evening spent at the only inn here will be memorable — the food is exquisite, if slightly adventurous, and the stars seem brighter than anywhere else.

Day 7: Shinchaya to O-tsumago
12.8 km (8 miles); 3 hours

A 45-minute walk takes you to one of the best-preserved post-towns on the route — Magome. Sitting in the hills above the Kiso Valley at 800 m (2,600 ft), its name means 'horse-basket', because this is where travellers were forced to leave their mounts before tackling the next mountainous stretch of the Nakasendo Highway. Home to Shimazaki Toson, one of Japan's most famous novelists, it is a fascinating place. From here, you make your way over the scenic Magome Pass before heading down to O-tsumago, a small collection of inns. You will have plenty of time to explore the area, in particular the mountain-top hot spring, before retiring to the Maruya Inn for dinner.

BLOSSOM LADEN CHERRY TREES LINE THE ROAD FROM TSUMAGO

Day 8: O-tsumago to Nojiri
23 km (14 miles), 5 hours; train to Suhara

Half an hour away from the enclave of O-tsumago lies the post-town Tsumago, which if anything is even more beautiful than Magome. No signs of the 21st century are apparent (television aerials, telephone and electricity lines are all hidden) and it is just like stepping back in time. It is essential to visit the museum, before making your way to the site of the former Tsumago Castle with its outstanding views of the Kiso Valley. After walking down to the modern town of Nagisio, you turn to the hills again for a walk through forests up to the station at Nojiri, where you catch a train to another post-town, Suhara.

Day 9: Train to Yabuhara via
Kiso-Fukushima; walk from Yabuhara to
Narai 14.5 km (9 miles), 3½ hours

After a quick trip to see Kiso-Fukushima (one of only two barrier towns on the highway, built so the authorities could monitor the passage of all travellers) you jump on the train to Yabuhara. Arriving here, you climb the Torii Pass and then follow the ancient path down to the village of Narai, passing a sacred Shinto shrine en route, until you reach your final guesthouse for the trip, in the centre of the village

Day 10: Train to Matsumoto, then to Nagoya.
Bullet train to Kyoto. Transfer to airport.

Contact: Walk Japan
www.walkjapan.com
TEL: +852 2817 6781 OR: +44 (0)1252 760 000
FAX: +852 2817 6781 OR: +44 (0)1252 760 001

Kenya is often said to be the cradle of mankind — the oldest remains of ancestral hominids to have been uncovered in the world so far have come from the shores of Lake Turkana, in the northeast of the country, close to the border with Ethiopia. Much of Kenya's early history is shrouded in the mists of time, although early tribespeople — the ancestors of the Pygmy and Bushman peoples of today — are thought to have lived as hunter gatherers, moving from place to place according to the seasons. There were probably fewer than 100,000 people living in an area of land roughly two and a half times the size of Britain.

- Route rating: moderate
- 14 days/13 nights
- Dates: February and October

Masai Mara to Mount Kenya to Lamu, Kenya

The population of contemporary Kenya numbers over 30 million and is made up of more than 30 different ethnic groups, which has led to great divisions and internal strife. Ethnicity is broadly divided between the pastoral people (including the Masai and the Samburu tribes) who herd livestock and live relatively nomadic lives, and the agriculturalists, the Kikuyu, who have prospered owing to their ability to compete in modern markets with cash crops such as cut flowers, tobacco and vegetables. However, of all the tribespeople the Masai are probably the most famous — with their majestic bearing, cloaks of scarlet and complex beaded jewellery, they are renowned for their bravery (killing a lion is the test of manhood), and their traditional diet of cow's milk and blood taken from the jugulars of living beasts. Sadly, modern life and all that it involves — the concept of land ownership, tourism, education, cash — is greatly eroding the Masai's long-established culture. The geography of Kenya ranges from lowland rainforests, wooded savannahs and coastal mangrove swamps to highland forests, snow-capped mountains and desert bushland. Its beautiful terrain is filled with more than a hundred species of large native mammals, including elephants, giraffes, lions, leopards, gazelle, zebras, rhinos and hippopotamuses, to name but a few. Flamingos, ostriches, herons, marabou and kingfishers are some of 1,070 bird species found in the country. Taking you from tribal areas of the Masai Mara to the predominantly Muslim Lamu archipelago, with a visit to Mount Kenya and the territory of the Samburu in between, this trip offers you a flavour of Kenya's diverse cultures and terrain. Your routine follows the customs of the local people and wildlife — rising with the sun and setting off at 6.30am most days, taking a siesta in the middle of the day and then walking again when it is cooler after 5pm. As you will be tracking animals for some of the time, khaki or sandy-coloured clothes are a good idea, and wear long trousers to protect your legs from thorns. As with all hot countries, taking precautions against sunburn is essential. Although Kenya is an equatorial country, most of your time is spent at altitude, 1,500–1,800 m (5,000–6,000 ft), so temperatures in February and October (the best times to travel) should not go above 29°C (85°F).

Day 1: Fly from Wilson Airport (Nairobi) to Masai Mara (private plane), 45 minutes; transfer to Cottars 1920s Camp, 30 minutes

The short flight from Wilson Airport provides you with stunning views of the Great Rift Valley before you arrive in Kenya's most famous game reserve, the Masai Mara. Staying deep in the bush at the secluded Cottars 1920s Camp, you sleep in luxurious antique-filled tents, evocative of early 20th-century colonial living. An evening game drive in open-sided jeeps should take you past elephants, zebra and antelope browsing near waterholes, before you return for a traditional sundowner (drink) and dinner.

Day 2: Stalking in Ol Koroi Valley 13km (8 miles), 6 hours

Leaving the camp early, you follow local hunters through the bush as they stalk lion, leopard, giraffe and elephants. Breakfasting on the top of the Sekanani Ridge, you are surrounded by magnificent views which span the length of the Masai Mara. After walking to the end of the ridge, you return to the camp for lunch and a siesta. This evening's drive takes you on a new route, along which you may come across lions and hyenas.

Day 3: Tracking in Ol Koroi Valley and walk to Mara Fly Camp
11.4km (7 miles), 5½ hours;
Following animal paths in the bush, you are taught how to identify different sets of tracks from giraffe to ostrich, as well as how to tell the age of an elephant by its dung; you will also discover which plants have healing properties. After arriving at the Mara Fly Camp on the Sand River in time for lunch, you spend the early evening walking in the National Park and visiting a Masai village.

Day 4: Walk along the Sand River
13km (8 miles); 5½ hours
Walking along the Sand River, where many animals come to drink, and then up to the Ol Entoroto Ridge, you will enjoy wonderful views of the African plains stretching as far as Tanzania. The afternoon is spent relaxing at the Fly Camp – so called because it is a mobile camp set up especially for the trip. Masai warriors are on duty throughout the night to protect you from any curious wild animals.

Day 5: Fly from Masai Mara to the foot of Mount Kenya (private plane), 2 hours
After a final morning game drive in the Masai Mara and a picnic lunch, you have a scenic flight which takes you over the Mau Escarpment, flamingo-fringed Lake Nakuru and the Laikipia Plateau to the exclusive Borana Ranch at the foot of Mount Kenya. You can cool off in the swimming pool before relaxing in the shade of an acacia tree to enjoy the panoramic views of this breathtaking mountain, the second highest in Africa at 5,200 m (17,060 ft).

THE MAU ESCARPMENT

Day 6: Free day at Mount Kenya

After the hectic but exciting schedule of the past few days, you can spend the day chilling out by the pool, or you can enjoy these awe-inspiring surroundings at closer quarters by going fishing, walking or riding.

Day 7: Drive from Mount Kenya to Lewa Wildlife Conservancy, 30 minutes; fly to the Northern Frontier District, 30 minutes; walk to camel safari camp 4.8 km (3 miles), 2 hours

In the 1950s there were over 65,000 black rhino in Africa, but by the late 1980s poaching had hacked this number down to 2,000. Around 40 rhinos, both black and white, live in the safety of the Lewa Wildlife Conservancy. Here you can observe these endangered creatures before flying to the rugged territory of the Samburu tribes people in the Northern Frontier District. A gentle walk through the bush, accompanied by Samburu herders, takes you to a picturesque campsite where the tents are made of mosquito-netting, allowing you to watch the vast celestial panorama from the comfort of your bed.

Days 8–11: Camel train in the Northern Frontier District 14.5–17.7 km (9–11 miles), 5–6 hours per day

Exploring the unspoilt country around the Mathews and Ndoto Mountain Ranges, which rise abruptly up to 2,700 m (9,000 ft) from the surrounding semi-arid plains, you taste the nomadic lifestyle of the Samburu – a tribe similar to the Masai, who have started to herd camels alongside cows to combat the ravages of drought. Your days assume a gentle routine – up early in the morning to catch the wildlife and avoid the heat, lunch and then a long siesta before an evening walk while the camp is being set up (you choose where your tent is placed depending on how much seclusion you like). A train of camels carries all the equipment, personal luggage, food and water for the trip. Dinner is served by candlelight, under the stars, and you are lulled to sleep by the soft chimes of the camel bells.

SAMBURU NATIONAL RESERVE

Day 12: Fly from the Northern Frontier District to Lamu, 2 hours

The small island of Lamu is situated off the upper east coast of Kenya. Once known as a hippie hang-out (it took over from Marrakech in the 1970s), it still retains a gloriously laid-back atmosphere. Surrounded by an azure sea, it has pristine beaches and is protected from the Indian Ocean by a coral reef. Staying at the exclusive Peponi Hotel in the ancient village of Shela, you are treated with delicious fresh seafood and wonderful views out to sea.

Day 13: Free day in Lamu

Lamu was first populated by Arab traders in the 12th century, and the island retains strong Muslim traditions. It is worth allowing some time to wander around the quaint streets to view the unique architecture; the Lamu Museum is one of the best in Kenya. In the afternoon you can take a boat trip out to the reef, which teems with colourful fish, or try snorkelling before returning to the comforts of the Peponi.

Day 14: Late afternoon return flight to Nairobi, 2 hours

Contact: ATG Oxford
www.atg-oxford.co.uk
TEL: +44 (0)1 865 315 678
FAX: +44 (0)1 865 315 697

The High Atlas mountains, south of Marrakech, are the North African equivalent of the Himalayas. They form a jagged mountainous desert, interspersed with emerald-green valleys, where the panoramic views are awe-inspiring. Strangely coloured rock formations jump out at you as you follow the myriad dusty tracks that have crisscrossed the area for centuries.

• Route rating: moderate
• 8 days/7 nights
• Dates: all year round

Marrakech to the Ourika Valley, Morocco

The mountains are home to the Berbers, a North African tribe who took refuge from the Arabs in this boulder-strewn wilderness in the 7th century. For years the area remained unexplored by Europeans, and it was only in the second half of the 19th century that a systematic exploration of the various ranges began. In today's world, the Berbers in the remote mountain villages eke out a simple existence through agriculture and tourism, their lives remaining relatively untouched so far by western culture. To make the most of this trip through the Toubkal region, it is best to hire a Berber guide and his mule: the beast will transport your luggage, while your guide will ensure that you don't get lost, aren't ripped off and always have food and a place to sleep. Few Berbers speak much English, but a good proportion speak passable French; they are renowned for being generous hosts and are friendly towards travellers.

The Toubkal region, which includes the highest peak in North Africa, Jbel Toubkal, 4,167 m (13,670 ft), is one of the most popular destinations for walkers because of its imposing scenery and accessibility from Marrakech. The route for this particular trip, from Aremd to Timichi, is a relatively easy walk. It is passable all year round, but in winter there are often substantial snow falls which make progress far more difficult. In July and August, midday temperatures can reach 35°C (95°F); the most benign months are May, June and October.

While the physical aspects of this holiday are not too taxing, it certainly provides a memorable adventure. However, be warned – this is not sophisticated western travelling. The food you are given is simple, fairly repetitious, but healthy; the places you stay at are clean, but basic. Bathrooms are rarely en suite, and you need to bring a three-season sleeping bag with you for your nights in the gîtes (Berber-run refuges). Most importantly, you must take a broad-brimmed sunhat, plenty of sunscreen and iodine drops or purifying tablets to treat the water. Where possible, try to wear lightweight trousers and long-sleeved cotton shirts; out of respect to Muslim culture, women should keep their arms and legs covered and avoid wearing tight clothing.

TRADITIONAL TERRACED FIELDS IN THE ARID ATLAS MOUNTAINS

Day 1: Marrakech

If your flight times allow you to arrive in Marrakech by mid-afternoon, you will have time to explore one of the city's most famous landmarks — the Djemaa-el-Fna. This huge square in the old part of the city comes alive at night and is a source of endless entertainment with its jugglers, snake-charmers, musicians, acrobats and story-tellers. You can observe this colourful scene from the Restaurant Argana, at the same time as sampling the delicious cuisine. The hotel Riad Magi has an English owner and is conveniently situated within walking distance of Djemaa el-Fna. Its central courtyard, which is filled with orange trees and fountains, provides a peaceful retreat from the hectic streets.

Day 2: Drive from Marrakech to Imlil, 1½ hours; Imlil to Aremd 3.4 km (2 miles), 35 minutes

The drive out of Marrakech takes you past the Royal Palace and on through the dusty Hoaz plains to the spectacular gorges at Moulay Brahim. After the town of Asni, where Winston Churchill enjoyed painting holidays, the tarmac peters out and there is a slightly bumpy ride until you reach Imlil 17 km (10½ miles) further on. This is where the road ends, and from here you walk through walnut terraces to the hill village of Aremd. From the newly built Hotel Aremd you have outstanding views of the towering peak of Jbel Toubkal. If you have time, it is worth visiting the local *hammam* (Moroccan version of a sauna) and having a massage.

Day 3: Circular walk to Sidi Chamarouch 10 km (6 miles), 3½ hours

Having breakfasted on the terrace, surrounded by almond trees, ask the hotel for a packed lunch. Make sure you have a full water bottle with you (only buy bottles with the seal intact or drink soft drinks, which are readily available). Following the most popular route up to Toubkal, you pass through apple orchards before climbing the path to the higgledy-piggledy hamlet of Sidi Chamarouch. Developed around an ancient shrine, it is believed to have healing powers. Walking along a nearby stream you will find a secluded spot with some small waterfalls, which is an ideal stopping point for lunch. Once refreshed, it is time to turn round and make your way back to Aremd, where you can look forward to a healthy dinner of couscous, or vegetable and lamb *tagine*.

Day 4: Aremd to Tacheddirt 12 km (7½ miles), 5 hours

Ideally, it is a good idea to start walking before 8am so that by midday, when the sun is at its most powerful, you can stop and find some shade. After making your way back down to Imlil, you head on to the village of Tamatert, with its characteristic flat-roofed earthen dwellings. From here you climb up to the Tizi n'Tamatert pass, 2,279 m (7,520 ft), where you can stop off to enjoy the view and buy soft drinks from a weather-beaten shack that doubles as a café. The view of the valley below is stunning, and at the far end you can see the village of Tacheddirt, your final destination. This evening you stay in a gîte, where you can sleep either indoors or outside on a terrace under a sky renowned for its celestial clarity.

Day 5: Tacheddirt to Oukaimedene
10.8 km (6½ miles), 4½ hours

Breakfast in the gîte normally consists of fresh unleavened bread and jam, with tea or coffee. Before setting off early again (the Berber day runs from 6am to 6pm), you can request a packed lunch, and remember to take lots of water with you. You start the long, dusty climb, past terraces of wheat, barley and maize, up the zigzags to the pass at Tizi nou Addi, 2,960 m (9,768 ft). In front of you, the two towers of Djebel Anngour, 3,616 m (11,932 ft), shoot upwards to dominate the skyline. This is a good place to eat your packed lunch, before starting the gradual descent to the skiing village of Oukaimedene. The landscape grows progressively more fertile, and in the summer months, as you wander along the sides of meadows, you find you are walking past a large apiary: the noise of the bees is deafening. In the skies above, you should be able to spot eagles, kites and falcons wheeling gracefully. If you have any energy left when you arrive in Oukaimedene, 'the meeting place of the four winds', ask your guide to show you the nearby prehistoric rock carvings. Chez JuJu is one of the most comfortable places to stay, and is one of the very few hotels where you can order a beer.

Day 6: Oukaimedene to Timichchi
12km (7½ miles), 5 hours

This is a relatively hard day's walking, so make sure you have plenty of water with you and remember to ask for your packed lunch. Two and a half hours after leaving the village on a good mule path, you will arrive at the top of Tizi nou Attar which, at 3,260 m (10,758 ft), is the highest point of the trip. As you descend into the beautiful Ourika Valley, one of the most scenic and least visited passages in the Atlas Mountains, the colours around you change from sandy yellow to red and then to green. Walking past the villages of Agounss and Tinoummer you finally arrive at the friendly gîte in Timichchi.

Day 7: Timichchi to Setti Fadma
11 km (7 miles), 4 hours;
drive to Marrakech 1 hour

The descent from Timichchi is very straightforward. From a track high above the valley you gain bird's-eye views down over the intricate irrigation channels and village terraces below. The path becomes increasingly rocky the closer you get to Setti Fadma, a small village spread out along the banks of a river. On Saturdays it has a bustling market, which is particularly crowded in summer and slightly jarring after the peace of the mountains. (Setti Fadma is a popular destination for people escaping the searing heat in Marrakech.) You should be back in Marrakech by mid-afternoon, which will give you time for more sightseeing or shopping in the *souk* at Djemma-el-Fna.

Day 8: Journey home from Marrakech.

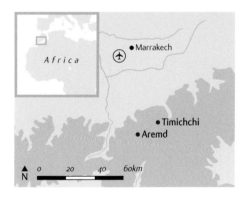

Contact: Sherpa Expeditions
www.sherpaexpeditions.com
TEL: +44 (0)20 8577 2717
FAX: +44 (0)20 8572 9788

The word 'enchantment' conjures up images of mystery, magic and fascination, or in short, an other-worldliness that is hard to pin down. However, it is an appropriate description for America's southern state of New Mexico. Dubbed the Land of Enchantment, its arid country is bathed in a soft light which has bewitched artists, writers and travellers for many generations.

- Route rating: easy—moderate
- 8 days/7 nights
- Dates: June to September

Taos to Santa Fe, New Mexico

The first thing to strike you about New Mexico is its size — everything seems so big: the skies, the high desert plains, the snow-capped peaks of the north. You can't help but experience a sense of awe combined with a feeling of insignificance in the face of such natural beauty. This is a land suffused with a strong sense of heritage — nowhere else in the States is there such a long history of continuous habitation. The first settlers, nearly one thousand years ago, were Native American Indians, collectively known as the Ancestral Puebloans. They built multistorey *pueblos* (houses) and astonishing cliff dwellings, before being ousted by ancestors of the modern day Pueblo Indians (*pueblo* is a Spanish word meaning village). Spanish missionaries arrived in the 1600s, and despite intermittent skirmishes the two cultures have continued to live side by side for nearly four hundred years.

The result has been an extraordinary fusion of Hispanic and Indian cultures, which was hardly dented by the arrival of Anglo-Americans in the 1800s. The Spaniards improved upon the original adobe-style of architecture (using hand-made bricks made from earth, sand, charcoal and chopped grass plastered over with a mixture of mud and straw) used by the Pueblos. Today, adobe architecture is still the defining feature of most buildings, from churches to shopping malls, right across the state. Meanwhile, the Pueblos adopted aspects of Catholicism which they mixed with their traditional beliefs and practices. As a result, they celebrate a unique combination of saint's days and national holidays such as the 4th July, along with ancient Native American rituals; their vibrant festivities are characterized by costumed dances and huge communal feasts.

Concentrating on the north of New Mexico, between the famous towns of Santa Fe and Taos, you explore the mysterious ruins of a prehistoric culture, as well as trekking through the vast sage-covered plains, flecked with purple and pink wildflowers. With summer temperatures varying between 21°C (70°F) and 28°C (82°F), walking conditions rarely grow uncomfortable. However, as you spend much of your time during this trip at an altitude of 2,134 m (7,000 ft), it is essential that you keep yourself well hydrated and take things easy to avoid falling prey to altitude sickness.

ANCESTRAL PUEBLOAN RUINS IN THE BANDELIER NATIONAL MONUMENT

Day 1: Arrival in Santa Fe

A 90-minute drive takes you from Albuquerque International Airport to Santa Fe. Staying at La Posada de Sante Fe, you will be able to enjoy Spanish colonial elegance at its best; if you are feeling slightly jet-lagged, a massage in the hotel's Avanyu Spa should help rejuvenate you.

Day 2: Drive to Tsankawi prehistoric ruins, 45 minutes; walk round ruins 2.6 km (1½ miles), 1 hour; drive to Taos, 1.5 hours; sightseeing at Taos Pueblo, 2 hours

Set in the foothills of the Jemez Mountains, the Bandelier National Monument is dotted with woodland and has a back drop of pink-hued canyons. Tsankawi forms a part of the monument and features the isolated remains of an ancient settlement, once three storeys high. Walking along the same trail that the Ancestral Puebloans trod, you find that parts of the path have been worn down waist-deep into the volcanic tuff. (The area's characteristic soft rock was created a million years ago, after gigantic volcano eruptions obliterated 1,036 sq km (400 sq miles) of land underneath 300 m (1,000 ft) of ash. The ash solidified into an easily eroded rock known as tuff.)

Driving north to Taos Pueblo, you visit a traditional adobe housing complex that has been lived in continuously for eight hundred years. Remaining largely unchanged since the Spanish first encountered it in 1540, the complex still lacks basic amenities including running water and electricity. Spending the night in the small town of Taos at the Casa Benavides B&B, you can enjoy the best of southern hospitality.

ANCESTRAL PUEBLOAN CLIFF DWELLINGS

Day 3: Drive to Wild Rivers Recreation Area, 1 hour; Rio Grande Gorge Loop 12.5 km (8 miles), 3½ hours

Descending 240 m (800 ft) into the Rio Grande Gorge, a volcanic canyon that runs for 96 km (60 miles) through New Mexico, you have the chance to spot some of the area's wildlife, including red-tailed hawks and prairie dogs. Prickly pear cacti and sagebrush line the route as you pass the thundering confluence of the Red River and the Rio Grande. From here, you walk a little further to find some ancient petroglyphs before starting the steep climb out of the gorge. Back in Taos in the evening, it is well worth visiting the Appletree Restaurant, where the mango chicken *enchiladas* are a speciality.

Day 4: Drive to La Cueva Lake, 1 hour; walk 11.4 km (7 miles), 3½ hours

After the starkness of the high desert plateau, the green of the Carson National Forest seems particularly verdant. After wandering around the lake, you climb to the top of La Cueva Peak for some magnificent views of the Sangre de Cristo Mountains. Afterwards, a short drive takes you to Chimayó, a mountain village famous for its weavers and the Sanctuario de Chimayó. This 1812 Spanish colonial church is an important pilgrimage destination, known as the Lourdes of America. People flock to the church in the hope that by rubbing some of its holy earth onto their bodies they will be cured of their ailments. Walking to the centre of the village and staying at the Rancho de Chimayó, you will be treated to some of the best traditional cuisine in the north of New Mexico.

THE SANDIA MOUNTAINS

Day 5: Drive to Bandelier National Monument, 30 minutes; Frijoles Canyon Trail 18.4 km (11½ miles), 4½ hours

It's a long day of walking, so make the most of breakfast before the short drive back to Bandelier National Monument. This time, head for the heart of the monument, where you come across a fascinating complex of cliff dwellings dug into the soft volcanic rock of Frijoles Canyon by Ancestral Puebloans. Following the creek along the bottom of the canyon, under the shade of cottonwood and pines, you make your way to the Ceremonial Cave. Situated in a rocky overhang 43 m (140 ft) above the canyon floor this is accessible only via a series of rickety ladders. Continuing along the path, you come to the Long House — a 240 m (800 ft) series of two- and three-storey adobe houses that contain a number of fascinating petroglyphs. After exploring the remains of Tyuonyi, a circular multistorey village, you will be ready to make your way into Sante Fe and the irresistible luxury of the Inn of the Anasazi.

Day 6: Santa Fe

One of America's oldest and most beautiful cities, Santa Fe is a wonderful place to explore. Built over the ruins of an abandoned Pueblo settlement in the early 1600s, the city has strict construction laws that require that all modern buildings have to replicate the original Spanish colonial architecture. The result is that it is often extremely difficult to tell which adobe buildings originate from the 17th century and which were built in the 20th. Starting your day in the central plaza, make your way across to the Palace of the Governors, which houses a vast array of artefacts that highlight the region's colourful history. The Museum of Fine Arts, St Francis Cathedral (built of stone and not adobe), the Museum of Indian Arts and Culture, and the San Miguel Mission (the oldest church in America to have remained in continuous use) are all fascinating places to visit, along with the scores of galleries and shops for which Santa Fe is famous. In the Anasazi Restaurant you can expect to be served such delicacies as blue corn dusted scallops or flash-fried calamari with chilli.

Day 7: Atalaya Mountain walk
10.6 km (7 miles), 3 hours

A short car journey back into the high desert takes you to the Atalaya Mountain trailhead. From here it is a 534 m (1,780 ft) climb to the summit, where you find panoramic views of the Jemez Mountains to the west and the Sandia Mountains to the south. Walking back down, you can find welcome shade under the branches of the surrounding juniper, Douglas fir and ponderosa pine trees. After a picnic lunch, you can spend the rest of the afternoon exploring Santa Fe or enjoying the sybaritic facilities offered by one of the city's many top class spas.

Day 8: Return to Albuquerque International Airport

THE SAN JUAN MOUNTAINS

Contact: Backroads
www.backroads.com
TEL: +1 510 527 1555
FAX: +1 510 527 1444

Its inhabitants refer to it as 'Godzone' — in other words, God's own country. While New Zealanders may be taking hyperbole to its furthest limit, they have got a point.

- Route rating: easy—fairly strenuous
- 10 days/9 nights
- Dates: December to March

Arthur's Pass to Lake Wanaka, New Zealand

Just over 1,500 km (900 miles) from the nearest landmass (Australia), New Zealand is a huge unspoilt, natural adventure playground made up of primeval forests, jaw-dropping mountains, volcanic pools and glacier-fed lakes. It is an adrenaline junkie's dream world — the fast-flowing rivers are perfect for white-water rafting, the snow-capped alpine mountains make excellent ski-resorts and its national parks (which make up one-third of its landscape) are crisscrossed with some of the best hiking trails imaginable. In fact, walking in the bush ('tramping' as the New Zealanders refer to it) isn't just a pastime here, it's a way of life, and few people live more than a short drive from some form of pristine bushland.

Consisting of two islands (north and south), New Zealand has a landmass only slightly bigger than Britain's and yet has a population of just under 4 million people — a quarter of whom live in the largest city, Auckland. This means that a huge area of the country is dominated purely by nature and not by man. The New Zealanders (most of whom are of British or Polynesian descent) are extremely protective of their natural inheritance and are justifiably proud of the country's renowned eco-systems. Thousands of years of geographic isolation have protected New Zealand from over-population and over-development, and have also led to the birth of some extraordinary species of flora and fauna, including kea (alpine parrot), kakapo (huge ground-dwelling parrot) and the flightless kiwi bird, while the variety of vegetation is simply enormous. There are no indigenous mammals in New Zealand, but many new species (rabbits, possums, horses, sheep, pigs, dogs, deer and cattle) have been introduced by settlers.

Based purely on South Island, this trip takes you from one extreme to another; from subtropical forests to glaciers and snow-capped mountains to sun-kissed beaches. The summer months (December to March) provide optimum walking conditions, with temperatures around 22°C (72°F). It will undoubtedly rain while you are in the mountains (the Southern Alps, the spine down the middle of the island, don't just attract bad weather, they make it!). However, the main hazard you need to prepare for is sunburn. The sun shines more fiercely here than in the northern hemisphere and New Zealand has a high rate of skin cancer. Don't be tempted to sunbathe between 11am and 3pm, always wear sunscreen and bring a hat with you.

MOUNT COOK

THE SOUTHERN ALPS

Day 1: Drive from Christchurch to Castle Hill, 90 minutes
Optional walk in Craigieburn Forest Park 4–8 km (3–5 miles), 1–2 hours

The drive from Christchurch, on the east coast, up to Craigieburn Forest Park (near the famous Arthur's Pass) in the centre of the island is characterized by vast geographical contrasts, ranging from coastal plains through fertile farmland to mountain ski resorts. Walking around the park on any one of the many tracks through the beech forests, alpine scrub and tussock grasslands, you see a wealth of native plants including scarlet mistletoe and hebe. The birdlife is stupendous, and you soon come into contact with the gregarious keas, long-tailed cuckoos and many others. A short drive takes you to Wilderness Lodge, a luxurious and secluded retreat, which doubles up as a working sheep station.

Day 2: Wilderness Lodge to Bealey Spur
8 km (5 miles), 3 hours
On a guided walk with one of the Lodge's knowledgeable naturalists, you slowly climb through a beech forest up to an alpine lake with excellent views of the surrounding snow-capped mountains. If you are lucky, you may see patches of South Island edelweiss. However, you should have no problem spotting examples of New Zealand's smallest bird, the rifleman, as well as grey warblers, bellbirds and silver eyes. The Lodge also organizes a guided night-sky walk on which constellations such as the Southern Cross and Orion are pointed out to you.

Day 3: Drive to Point Elizabeth Walkway,
1.5 hours and walk 4 km (2½ miles), 1 hour; Porarri Punakaiki Loop 8 km (5 miles), 2½ hours
After walking for a stretch along the island's west coast, through flax and rimu trees coated in spray from the Tasman Sea, it's a quick drive to the seaside town of Punakaiki, made famous by its unique geological curiosities — the Pancake Rocks and Blowholes. Walking in the lush forest by the Porarri River after lunch, you are dwarfed by massive tree ferns and huge rata trees. The track leads you directly to the Punakaiki Rocks Hotel, which has delightful views along the beach.

Day 4: Drive to Hari Hari Coastal Walkway,
2 hours; walk (4½ miles), 2½ hours
As you drive south along the coast, the landscape changes from arable farmland to temperate vegetation where sphagnum moss lies at the roadside. The Hari Hari Coastal Walkway is a 19th-century miner's trail, which leads you through a kahikatea forest — New Zealands tallest species of tree. You emerge at Doughboy Point, where you can admire fabulous views of the Southern Alps and the Tasman Sea. A short drive brings you to the Franz Josef Glacier Hotel, perfectly situated in a rainforest within sight of the eponymous glacier.

LAKE WANAKA

Day 5: Waiho Valley walk
7.4 km (4½ miles), 2½ hours

With ice on one side and abundant vegetation on the other, the Franz Josef Glacier is one of the world's few temperate rainforest glaciers. Walking beneath lichen-laden trees in the Waiho Valley you see a perfect example of how plant life quickly colonizes the land behind a receding glacier. The glacier itself is riven with deep blue crevasses and remote ice caves, which you can choose to explore after being dropped off by helicopter.

Day 6: Lake Matheson and Fox Glacier
4.3 km (3 miles), 1½ hours

Any book on New Zealand invariably has a picture of Mount Cook (New Zealand's highest peak at 3,754 m (12,316 ft) and Mount Tasman reflected in the waters of Lake Matheson. A short drive brings you to this memorable spot where, after a wander along the lakeshore, you follow a track leading up to the Chalet Lookout. The views from this observation point over Fox Glacier, with its impressive rock falls, are tremendous. A one-hour drive brings you to the award-winning Wilderness Lodge Lake Moeraki, located on the edge of the lake and surrounded by forest.

Day 7: Lake Moeraki, optional walk 5.6 km (3½ miles), 2 hours

There is a wealth of different options to choose from today: this whole area has been designated a World Heritage Site, and you can either explore the unspoilt forest on foot or take a guided canoe trip around tranquil Lake Moeraki. Equally, you could follow a track that starts close to the Lodge and meanders beside a stream to lead you to Monro Beach, from where you can observe fur seals and penguins.

Day 8: Jet boat ride followed by Haast Pass Bridle Track; Lake Wanaka walk 8 km (5 miles), 2½ hours

Leaving the west coast and heading inland to the Haast River, you hop on a jet boat for a 14.5 km (9 mile) ride into the heart of the mountains for a trip that is both informative and exhilarating, as you pass high cliffs, thunderous waterfalls and dense forests. Walking down from Haast Pass, 563 m (1,847 ft), you find that the landscape has changed again — this time to tussock, scrub and beech forest. After following an old pioneer track down to Davis Flat, there's an hour's drive to the small town of Lake Wanaka, from where you wander along the lake to the front door of the Edgewater Resort Hotel.

Day 9: Free day in Wanaka

Wanaka bills itself as an adventure destination, and if you are seeking thrills, you won't be disappointed. Jet boating, horse riding, rock climbing, parapenting and kayaking are all on offer. There are also a number of spectacular walks, including a sunrise hike up Mount Iron, 2 km (1½ miles), which takes you through kanuka woodland and offers panoramic views of Lake Wanaka and the surrounding countryside. If you don't feel like an uphill climb, you can take the lakeside path past Eely Point and on to Breacon Point. You should come across a wide variety of birds along this track, including parakeets and pukekos.

Day 10: Drive to Queenstown, 30 minutes

Making a slight detour on the way to the airport, you can finish (yourself) off with a scenic bungy jump over the Nevis River — at 134 m (440 ft), it's the highest in New Zealand and guaranteed to make you regret having eaten breakfast.

Contact: Backroads
www.backroads.com
TEL: +1 510 527 1555
FAX: +1 510 527 1444

In terms of scenic beauty, the West Highland Way is certainly one of the finest walks in Britain. Starting in the Lowlands of Scotland, a mere 11.4 km (7 miles) from the country's largest city, Glasgow, it stretches northwards for 152 km (95 miles) until it eventually reaches the historic town of Fort William, which sits at the head of Loch Linnhe. The landscape changes dramatically from open rolling countryside to barren heather moorland, and finally into the brooding peaks of the Grampian Mountains.

- Route rating: moderate
- 8 days/7 nights
- Dates: all year round

West Highland Way – Drymen to Fort William, Scotland

The path is not difficult to follow, nor is it particularly difficult to complete. It passes along a mixture of Land Rover tracks, estate drives and forestry roads, making it hard for you to get lost. Many of these tracks were originally ancient drovers' roads on which cattle were herded to market, although part of the path runs along an old military road built to help the troops control the Jacobite rebellions of the 18th century.

If you are lucky, you may glimpse a golden eagle as you travel north, and on Rannoch Moor you will almost certainly see red deer. However, the only wildlife with which you are likely to come into really close contact are midges. These small, mosquito-like insects are harmless but exceptionally irritating, so be sure to bring plenty of repellent with you.

Generally, you are advised to travel the West Highland Way from south to north, as this will mean that you have the sun at your back. It can usually be walked at any time of year, but in winter the path is often covered by snow and ice, making the trip considerably more hazardous. Waterproof, windproof and warm clothing is therefore recommended in the winter months, with layers for insulation, and walkers may find a metal-tipped walking stick useful if it gets snowy or icy. Freezing gales do not improve matters either. The best weather conditions are normally found in August and September, but these months also mark the shooting and stalking seasons, so it is important not to venture off the prescribed route.

It is almost impossible to fit the whole of the West Highland Way into a comfortable seven-day walk, so you may want to consider cutting out the early stage, which is essentially just a suburb of Glasgow, and instead begin several kilometres north of Milngavie, the official start.

LOCH LOMOND

Day 1: Drive from Glasgow to Drymen, 25 minutes

This version of Scotland's most popular and historic walk begins 24 km (15 miles) north of Glasgow, in the small village of Drymen — known as one of the gateways to the Highlands. It was once a haunt of the famous 17th-century brigand Rob Roy, who came to the village to collect his protection money from Lowland farmers. A 25-minute drive from Glasgow, your first night is spent in the cosy 17th-century Winnock Hotel, which is conveniently situated just across the square from the country's oldest pub, the Clachan. The hotel often holds ceilidhs at the weekends and provides a lively start to the trip.

THE WATERFALLS AT FALLOCH

Day 2: Drymen to Rowardennan/Inverbeg 22.4 km (14 miles); 5½ hours

Shaggy Highland cattle watch you with mild curiosity as you wind your way up over Conic Hill, with its panoramic views stretching from Stirling to Glasgow, and then down to Loch Lomond, the largest body of inland water in Britain. The loch is home to salmon, sea trout and brown trout, as well as freshwater herring. The latter are fairly rare in Britain and it is thought that they were left in the loch during sea-level changes after the last series of glaciations. The walking is easy-going, particularly on the undulating paths at the loch side, where you have the chance to see a staggering array of trees, wildflowers and ferns. At Rowardennan you make your way to the little pier for the ferry which takes you across the loch to the acclaimed Inverbeg Hotel, with its spectacular views and award-winning restaurant, where you can expect such delicacies as home-cured salmon or roast quail with apricot and walnut stuffing. If you are feeling really energetic you can climb Ben Lomond, Scotland's most southerly *Munro* (mountain over 914 m/3,000 ft).

Day 3: Inverbeg to Crianlarich
16 km (10 miles), 4½ hours

To fit this whole trip into a week and to avoid some pretty boring walking through endless Forestry Commission plantations, start the day with a taxi ride up to Ardlui, where you catch another ferry across the northern end of Loch Lomond to Ardleish. Here you rejoin the West Highland Way for an attractive walk up Glen Falloch, through farmland and woodlands and past waterfalls and peat-tinted streams. This part of the path was once a cattle drovers' track and the walking is generally straight-forward, although it can become more testing if the path is wet and muddy. The night is spent at the three-star Ben More Lodge, where the restaurant specializes in dishes using local products, in particular fresh game and fish.

Day 4: Crianlarich to Inveroran
25.5 km (16½ miles), 6½ hours

This is the longest day's walk but, if the idea of the distance horrifies you, it is possible to peel off earlier at the Bridge of Orchy, 22.4 km (14 miles) and hop into a taxi for the remainder of the trip. However, as it is downhill most of the way, the walking is not too exhausting. Passing through forestry plantations, rolling farmland and the famous ruins of St Fillan's Chapel, you will arrive at the magnificently bleak Rannoch Moor. There is minimal shelter here and the weather conditions are mercurial, so it is important to take lots of layers and waterproof clothing. However, the views are dramatic as you gaze into great corries once filled by glaciers; this day also provides the best opportunities for spotting red deer, which thrive in this remote location. The Inveroran Hotel, on the banks of Loch Tulla, provides a welcome resting place.

Day 5: Inveroran to Kings House Hotel
19.3 km (12 miles), 5 hours

Previously walking for the longest day, you now face the most testing day as you make your way across the western edge of Rannoch Moor. The scenery is outstanding, but the weather is usually foul. In the distance you can see the intimidating silhouette of Glencoe, infamous from the massacre of the MacDonalds by the Campbells in 1692. About 1.6 km (1 mile) from the foot of this unforgettable glen you come to the Kings House Hotel, which was once used as a barracks by soldiers of George III after the Battle of Culloden. It is considerably more hospitable and comfortable now which is lucky, because in this remote area it is the only available accommodation!

Day 6: Kings House Hotel to Kinlochleven
14.5 km (9 miles), 3½ hours

Short and sharp is the best way to describe today's walking. The exceptional beauty of the landscape provides a welcome distraction as you climb your way up the aptly named Devil's Staircase. Once at the top, however, the views are outstanding, and if the weather is clear you can see the outline of Ben Nevis in the distance. As you tackle the dramatic but knee-cracking descent to Kinlochleven it is easy to understand why Robert Louis Stevenson used it as the setting for his book *Kidnapped*. Kinlochleven itself is a fairly unmemorable little town, but continuing up the West Highland Way for another twenty minutes you come to Mamore Lodge. With its original Victorian wood panelling, bay-windowed dining room and extremely well-stocked bar, it is a particularly charming stop-off point.

Day 7: Kinlochleven to Fort William
22.4 km (14 miles), 6½ hours

The last leg of the trip follows Victorian hunting tracks and General Wade's old military road as you wind your way over Lairigmor Pass and through dense coniferous forest to Glen Nevis. It is worth the short detour after Blar a'Chaorainn to visit Dun Deardail, a Stone Age fort with vitrified walls, before the final push towards Fort William. From here onwards Scotland's highest peak, Ben Nevis, 1,344 m (4,408 ft), fills the skyline in front of you. The route ends at the Bridge of Nevis. From here you walk 1.6 km (1 mile) north of the town centre to the Glenlochy Guest House, a family-run B&B that provides a warm place for you to put your feet up after this 120 km (75 mile) wander through the Highlands.

Day 8: Journey home

PANORAMA OF RANNOCH MOOR WITH
LOCH BA IN THE FOREGROUND

CLOUDS HANG LOW OVER THE OMINOUS GLENCOE

Contact: Sherpa Expeditions
www.sherpaexpeditions.com
TEL: +44 (0)20 8577 2717
FAX: +44 (0)20 8572 9788

After the Duke of Wellington's army re-took the Spanish town of Ciudad Rodrigo from the French during the Peninsular War (1808–14), his soldiers dissolved into a violent frenzy, randomly vandalizing property and stealing anything they could get their hands on. When control was eventually re-established, the troops went out on parade wearing an extraordinary mix of clothes and jewellery, all of which had been purloined from the French. Wellington took one look at his men and said in disbelief, 'Who the devil *are* those fellows?'

- Route rating: easy
- 8 days/7 nights
- Dates: April to September

Extremadura
– Cáceres to Ciudad Rodrigo, Spain

This is only one of the colourful stories that characterize this hot and dusty region of Spain, the scene of endless battles from Roman times through to the Civil War (1936–1939). On the border of Spain and Portugal, Extremadura has a harshly beautiful landscape which is frighteningly under-populated. Abandoned farmsteads and hamlets, surrounded by olive groves gone to seed, are poignant reminders of a once fertile land now left to waste. However, it was the countryside's intrinsic harshness that was the cause of the area's brief golden age in the 15th and 16th centuries: a cruel land breeds hard men and Extremadura was the birthplace of many of Spain's greatest conquistadores, including Francisco Pizarro and Hernando Cortes, who brought great wealth back to their native soil and used it to embellish towns such as Trujillo and Cáceres.

The scent of eucalyptus, lavender and pine gently follows you, through fields, along river gorges and over barren sierra, as you walk from Extremadura across the border into the Beira Baixa region of Portugal for two nights, and then back again. Vultures and eagles soar high above, while closer to the ground, trees and rooftops vibrate with a multitude of birds including golden orioles, bee eaters, cuckoos, and azure-winged magpies. In April and May, wildflowers blaze brightly and the temperature rarely rises above a comfortable 21°C (70°F). In the height of summer it is too hot to walk, but by September the heat has died down to a pleasant 25°C (77°F).

The route you follow is the brainchild of Adam Hopkins and Gaby Macphedran, who discovered the best places to walk after long conversations with farmers, shepherds, smugglers and poachers. The result is a magical journey, on which you are accompanied by mules and horses to carry everything you need. As you wander from one historic site to another, Adam brings the past to life with compelling stories of the Peninsular War, while Gaby ensures that at every step of the way you are nourished with samples of the best food and wine in the region. All you need to do is bring a pair of binoculars and soak up the atmosphere.

Day 1: Arrive at Madrid airport; drive to Finca El Vaqueril, 4 hours

Either Adam or Gaby will pick you up from the airport and then drive you westwards to the remote guesthouse of Finca El Vaqueril, a 19th-century farmstead sitting proudly at the end of an 8 km (5 mile) drive and surrounded by 810 hectares (2,000 acres) of classic Extremaduran countryside. Granite boulders, the size of small cars, dot the landscape like surreal Henry Moore sculptures, while aged oak trees cast ephemeral shadows in the dwindling light of the day. In the evening at dinner you have a chance to sample the delights of home-reared and home-cooked food, along with some of the finest local wines.

Day 2: Finca El Vaqueril circuit 10.4 km (6½ miles), 2½ hours; historical tour of Cáceres, 2 hours

Walking around the estate, across fields sprinkled with wildflowers and interspersed with cork oaks (every nine years their trunks are stripped of bark from which cork is produced), you see black-leg pigs snuffling around the bottom of the trees in search of acorns. Along the way, you come across a small collection of Visigothic tombs dating from the 5th to the 8th centuries. After a relaxed lunch back at the farmhouse, a forty-five minute drive takes you to the ancient walled town of Cáceres for a guided walk by Adam which provides an insight into the town's history.

Moorish, Roman and conquistador influences merge to create an enchanting ambience, and as you meander along the cobbled streets swallows swoop all around and storks perch in straggly nests at the top of every tower. Back at Finca El Vaqueril, you can look forward to a dinner of suckling pig or lamb cooked with pimento and garlic.

THE RUGGED COUNTRYSIDE NEAR CACERES

ONE OF THE MANY OLIVE GROVES NEAR MONSANTO

Day 3: Drive to Salvaterra do Extremo (Portugal) 30 minutes; walk to Termas de Monfortinho 13 km (8 miles), 3½ hours

Meeting the pack horses in the beautiful village of Salvaterra do Extremo, you begin your day's walking by venturing up the valley of the Erges River, with its steep-sided gorges and densely vegetated banks. Passing through a varied landscape of oak and eucalyptus plantations, riverine grassland and open farmland, you also have time to absorb some outstanding panoramic views before you arrive at the relaxed Portuguese spa of Termas de Monfortinho, where you stay at the four-star Hotel Fonte Santa.

Day 4: Monsanto to Idhanha-a-Velha 8 km (5 miles); 2 hours

A day to relax, and the walk between Monsanto and Idhanha-a-Velha is optional, although it is still well worthwhile visiting them by car if you are feeling tired. Monsanto clings precariously to the bottom of a jumbled, boulder-strewn hill, and its steep, twisting streets are dominated by a 12th-century castle built by the Knights Templar. An easy walk through oak woods, olive groves and lemon trees brings you to Idhanha-a-Velha, once a prosperous Roman settlement and now groaning with archaeological and historical monuments, including a 13th-century Knights Templar tower built on a Roman temple, a Roman bridge and a cathedral constructed on a site of palaeo-Christian origin. Back at the Hotel Fonte Santa, you can reinvigorate any weary muscles with a massage in the spa or a swim in the picturesque pool.

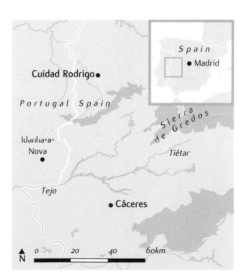

Day 5: Drive to the Spanish border, 30 minutes; walk to El Cabezo 19.3 km (12 miles), 4½ hours

Back on the Spanish side of the border, you are met by a cheerful muleteer and his donkeys. Winding your way over rolling farmland, with the hills of the Sierra de Gata directly ahead, you come across some of the abandoned and ruined farmsteads so common in this area. Slowly you move into a beautiful wilderness of overgrown fields and olive groves where, strangely, there are few visible animals, but scratched and disturbed bits of ground show where wild boar search for food. After a picnic lunch of Extremaduran ham, locally made sausages, cheese and fruit, you make your way to El Cabezo, a working farm with an enchanting guesthouse at the foot of the Sierra de Gata. If you don't wish to walk any further, vehicles will be available to take you to El Cabezo.

Day 6: Sierra de Gata circuit 11.4 km (7 miles), 2½ hours

The isolated Sierra de Gata is made up of a series of wooded hills and rocky outcrops – it is so remote that in some villages the locals still speak *Maniego*, a dialect made up of Portugese and Castilian Spanish. Walking along a rocky ridge, you can enjoy wonderful views of densely wooded valleys and small, stone-built hilltop villages. On your return to El Cabezo, you can accompany Miguel Garcia for a trip around his farm which includes 100 head of cattle, cork oaks and olive groves. The farm's home-produced olive oil is delicious and it is interesting to learn how the production process works.

THE MEDIEVAL TOWN OF CACERES

THE WALLED CITY OF CIUDAD RODRIGO

Day 7: El Cabezo to Hoyos
8 km (5 miles), 2½ hours;
drive to Ciudad Rodrigo, 40 minutes

Bidding farewell to El Cabezo, you make your way eastwards along the Sierra de Gata to the small village of Hoyos, where you can put your feet up and enjoy a sumptuous picnic laid out on a table under the shade of oak trees. After lunch, it's into the minibus for the drive into the historic walled city of Ciudad Rodrigo. Here the sleepy atmosphere belies the city's volatile past. Spanish, French, Portuguese and British armies all fought desperate battles here during the Peninsular War, and walking round its picturesque streets you can still find the marks of cannon shots peppered on many walls — in particular above one of the doors of the impressive Gothic cathedral, where you can see the distinctly painful dents left by cannon balls. Your final night is spent in a restored 14th-century castle, the Parador Nacional Enrique II, which is both comfortable and extremely evocative of times past.

Day 8: Return to Madrid, 4½ hour drive

Contact: The Ultimate Travel Company
www.walkeurope.com
TEL: +44 (0)20 7828 7778
FAX: +44 (0)20 7828 4856

Obliterated by concrete, heaving with semi-clothed post-adolescents and vibrating to the hypnotic beat of rave music; ask most people what they know about the Costa del Sol and that's the sort of answer you'll receive. Yet as soon as you venture inland – even just a short distance – you enter a parallel universe filled with rugged mountains, dramatic gorges, remote sierras, delightful villages and ancient castles.

- Route rating: easy
- 8 days/7 nights
- Dates: from April to September

The Ronda Safari – Gaucin to Ronda, Spain

Andalucía is a place of many contrasts. Lying in the far south of Spain, it is only a hair's breadth away from the northern tip of Africa and was the first region to be conquered by the Muslim invaders of the 8th century. Before long, almost all of the Iberian Peninsula had been taken over, and Andalucía became the seat of power for a new nation known as Al-Andalus (Muslim Spain). When Grenada, the last Muslim stronghold, eventually fell to the Christian Reconquista nearly 800 years later, in 1492, Andalucía was left with a rich Islamic heritage. This is still readily visible today in the form of magnificent architectural monuments such as the Mezquita in Córdoba and the Alhambra Palace in Grenada. On a more day-to-day level, Islamic culture still influences the region's cuisine, while two of Andalucía's most potent symbols – flamenco and the guitar – both originate from Islamic times.

Christianity brought superb Gothic, Renaissance and baroque architecture to the region, along with a fascinating folklore, although 200 years of economic stagnation have left rural Andalucía with an indisputable backward air. However, this backwardness is all part of the region's charm, and has bewitched generations of travellers including Byron, Mozart and Bizet, while its unspoilt landscape has provided inspiration for artists such as Velázquez, Murillo and Picasso.

The Ronda Safari takes you through a kaleidoscope of pristine scenery, from forests and green pastures near the Moorish village of Gaucin to the colossal limestone escarpments of the Roman city of Ronda (a mere hour from the Costa del Sol). The walking is gentle, and in the care of your guides cum hosts Hugh and Jane Arbuthnott, you are frankly spoilt rotten. Outstanding home-made cooking graces most meals, mid-morning breaks are characterized by glasses of ice-cold Fino and fresh lemonade, while afternoon siestas refresh you when temperatures rise to 28°C (82°F). A sun hat, light clothing, a thin waterproof jacket and something warm for the evenings should cover all climatic variations. A charming muleteer and his mules accompany you most walking days to carry your kit (and you, if you're feeling tired!). In the evenings, you are plied with some of the best wines in Spain, and throughout the trip there is always someone on hand to impart entrancing insights into the area's history and tradition.

THE MEDIEVAL CITY OF RONDA STANDING ABOVE THE EL TAJO GORGE

Day 1: Arrive at La Almuña

A 90-minute drive from Málaga airport brings you to La Almuña, a hill farm set in rolling countryside close to Gaucin. From the terrace of the honeysuckle-and-wisteria-clad farmhouse, you can see the Rock of Gibraltar on the horizon, and on a clear night a hint of the Atlas Mountains. There should be time for you to relax and take a walk in the woods or swim in the pool before dinner.

Day 2: La Almuña to Gaucin circuit
17.7 km (11 miles), 5 hours

Mildly curious sheep and goats pause in their eating as you stroll past on your way up through an ancient cork forest to an escarpment that conceals the dazzlingly white mountain village of Gaucin, perched on the crest of the Sierra del Hacho. Dominated by a Moorish fortress dating from the 9th century, the centre of the village is a tangle of narrow streets and higgledy-piggledy houses. After a leisurely lunch at a 200-year-old hotel, you begin the walk back to La Almuña through open country. The aroma of oregano, thyme and rosemary permeates the air, while eagles and griffon vultures cast shadows at your feet. If you don't feel up to the 6.4-km (4-mile) return journey, you can go back by car.

Day 3: La Almuña to Campamento de Castillejos 14.5 km (9 miles), 4½ hours

Accompanied by Pedro and his mules, you make your way down through cork and oak forest to the village of Cortes de la Frontera, the origins of which go back to the 11th century BC, although its current foundations were laid in the 16th century. From here you climb to a spacious African safari-style campsite, where a number of palatial tents (complete with pine-framed beds and marble washstands) are carefully arranged so that each has its own private view of the Llano de Libar mountains. Drinks are laid out on a linen-covered table, followed by a romantic candlelit dinner prepared by Jane Arbuthnott of shrimp bisque, grilled pork and aromatic local cheeses.

Day 4: Campamento de Castillejos, optional walk 8 km (5 miles), 3 hours

You may feel like spending the day in the secluded and peaceful surroundings of the tented camp and taking time out to read, write or paint. However, if you feel like exploring, a circular walk through the surrounding woods will showcase a wealth of flora and fauna, including mongoose and roe deer. The peeps, twitters, warbles and occasional shrieks of a wide variety of birdlife fill the air around you, and you should to be able to catch sight of hoopoes, bee eaters, shrikes and golden orioles before you return to the tents at the end of the day.

Day 5: Campamento de Castillejos to Cortijo Horcajo
20.8 km (13 miles), 6½ hours

Returning to Cortes de la Frontera, with its fig trees and pink snapdragons, you are served a traditional Spanish breakfast of pork fat on garlic toast, accompanied by cognac, in one of the local bars. Cognac at 7.30am may be a bit much for you, but it doesn't seem to deter the locals in the slightest. From here you set out across the Sierra de Libar, with the sound of the cicadas serenading you, until you reach the majestic Llano de Libar. This hidden plain of unparalleled beauty is concealed from the outside world by a series of pink limestone peaks. After sitting down in a meadow filled with celandine for a picnic of gazpacho, marinaded quail and chilled white wine, you can lie back on the cushions for a siesta. If you are now feeling too full to walk, a car will take you to Cortijo Horcajo, a stately 18th-century farmhouse standing below the Sierra de Grazelema. For those who feel like more exercise, it is a 9.6 km (6 mile) walk down from the mountains into the golden valley to Cortijo Horcajo, where you will be spending the next two nights.

Day 6: Cortijo Horcajo to Grazalema
11.4 km (7 miles), 4 hours

Walking in the impressive Sierra de Grazalema Natural Park, through oak woods and meadows brimming with dog roses and cornflowers, you come to the picture-postcard village of Grazalema. After a tapas lunch, you can wonder round the steep cobbled streets and perhaps visit one of the two beautiful 17th-century churches. Driving back to Cortijo Horcajo, you pass magnificent views of the great plain of the Guadalquivir River.

Day 7: Cortijo Horcajo to Ronda
11.4 km (7 miles), 4 hours

Barley fields and olive groves surround you as you make your way to the historic city of Ronda, branded as the home of bullfighting. Towering on a ridge 100 m (320 ft) above the dramatic El Tajo Gorge and engulfed by a ring of mountains, Ronda was built by the Romans and subsequently became the capital of a small Berber kingdom. Entering the city through the Arab quarter, La Ciudad, you arrive straight at the door of the Parador de Ronda, a stylish hotel perched right on the edge of the gorge. After having explored the bullring (one of the oldest in Spain), as well as the 14th-century Moorish Mondragón Palace and the 15th-century Church of the Sacred Spirit, you return to the Parador feeling more than ready to chill out in its cliff-top swimming pool.

Day 8: Return to Málaga airport, 1½ hours

Contact: The Ultimate Travel Company
www.walkeurope.com
TEL: +44 (0)20 7828 7778
FAX: +44 (0)20 7828 4856

Once one of the most volcanically active areas of Europe, Garrotxa — which means 'torn earth' — is now a peaceful and thinly populated area in the northeast of Spain, close to the border with France. The last eruption, at the Volcà del Croscat, took place 11,500 years ago, and since then natural erosion has softened the dormant volcanic cones into rounded hills, thickly covered with trees, lush meadows and fertile farmland.

Garrotxa — Rupit to Besalú, Spain

- Route rating: easy
- 8 days/7 nights
- Date: March to October

Garrotxa has a higher than average rainfall compared to surrounding areas and this, combined with the rich volcanic soil, has given birth to some outstanding forests, including the legendary beech wood of Fageda d'en Jorda, near Santa Pau. Evergreen oaks populate the lower slopes, but as the hills creep upwards and gradually start to transmogrify into the Pyrenees, deciduous oak and beech trees take over before giving way to sub-alpine meadows. There is a profusion of plant life, including some extremely rare species of wildflowers — Pyrenean milkwort with its large purple flowers and the pale pink-flowered gromwell. The forests are alive with a host of mammals, ranging from red squirrels to Etruscan shrews and wild boar.

The people of Cataluñya, which forms part of Garrotxa, are fiercely independent and speak Català, a language that Castilian (standard Spanish) speakers find hard to understand. The language and much of Cataluñyan culture were brutally suppressed under Franco's regime (1936–1975), but since the succession of King Juan Carlos, the area has firmly re-established its identity. Its cuisine is particularly distinct from that of the rest of Spain, and much of the country's best meat, including lamb and veal, hails from Garrotxa. Sausages and ham are particular specialities, along with deep-fried potatoes stuffed with minced pork. Delicious light white wines come from the Penedés region and full-bodied reds from the Emporda region.

Although walking trips in Garrotxa can be done at any time of year, in July the temperature can rise to 32°C (90°F), which makes exercise unpleasant; the ideal months are from March to May, as well as September and October. The terrain is gentle and you spend most of your time walking along farm and woodland tracks. Although the trees provide shade a lot of the time, the sun is extremely strong and you must come equipped with a broad-brimmed hat and sunscreen. Because of the midday heat, the locals take a long break over lunch and then carry on working until 8pm. It means dinner usually kicks off around 10pm, so don't be surprised if you find yourself the sole occupant of a restaurant at 8.30!

DENSELY FORESTED VOLCANIC CONES IN THE

PARC NATURAL DE LA ZONA DE LA GARROTXA

THE VIEW FROM LA SALUT

Day 1: Arrival in Rupit

After a 30-minute drive from Barcelona, you find yourself in the delightful village of Rupit, perched on the summit of a rocky, 840 m (2,750 ft) high, flat-topped mountain. Its old-world ambience is heightened by the quaint 16th-century stone and slate-roofed houses, twisting cobbled streets, baroque church and suspension footbridge. The three-star Hotel Estrella is situated in the village centre and has pretty views over the surrounding countryside.

Day 2: Rupit to La Salut
12.1 km (7½ miles), 3½ hours

Leaving Rupit you make your way past the Salt de Sallent, a dramatic 100 m (320 ft) waterfall. From here you follow paths up along the Collsacabra Ridge, which gives you magnificent views of the valleys and forests below. There are numerous viewpoints along the way, although one or two are pretty vertiginous and should be avoided if you are likely to feel wobbly. Leaving the ridge, you walk through rolling pastures and then into beech woods, before descending very gently into the sanctuary of Nuestra Seora de la Salut, 1,000 m (3,270 ft). A centre of devotions for hundreds of years, the sanctuary developed in the late 17th century. From its balconies and those of the nearby Hotel la Salute, the panorama of Garroxta, which includes the Hostoles Valley directly below, is breathtaking.

Day 3: La Salut to Joanetes
16 km (10 miles), 5½ hours

Walking out of Salut and back up through the woodlands, you rejoin the Collsacabra Ridge. The path takes you to the castle of Sant Miquel de Falgars, perched high on a rocky outcrop. After taking some time out to explore it, stop and have lunch before tackling the descent through thick woodland to the village of Joanetes. Along the way, you pass the main town of the Garrotxa region, Olot, which is fringed by four coned volcanoes. El Ferres, a family-run hotel in a refurbished 18th-century farmhouse near the centre of Joanetes, is highly recommended.

Day 4: Joanetes to Santa Pau
19 km (12 miles), 6½ hours

Following a series of quiet country lanes, you enter the Parc Natural de la Zona de la Garrotxa. There are about 30 volcanic cones in this 120 sq km (46 sq mile) park, the highest of which reaches 160 m (525 ft) and the widest measures 1.5 km (1 mile) across its base. There is something mildly surreal about this thickly wooded landscape, which dips and curves abruptly. The lanes undulate through the Fageda d'en Jorda, and if you are lucky you may see a wryneck or a hawfinch; you will almost certainly hear great spotted woodpeckers somewhere in the boughs of the surrounding beeches. Coming out of the forest, you arrive in the medieval village of Santa Pau. The three-star Hotel Cal Sastre, located just outside the village walls, not only has 10 antique-furnished bedrooms, but its sister-restaurant in the old part of the village serves some of the best food in the area.

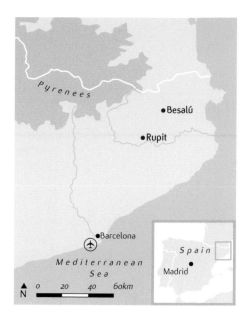

SANTA PAU

Day 5: Circular walk round Santa Pau
11.9 km (7½ miles), 3 hours

Santa Pau is an ancient barony with a castle founded in the 11th century. Its perimeter walls hide a charming village, bedecked with flower-filled balconies, modern sculptures and huge potted plants. Its simple Romanesque church of Santa Maria, built in the 15th century, usually opens at weekends. The circular walk from Santa Pau takes you past some of the most interesting parts of the Parc Natural, including the Santa Margarida crater, which has a tiny chapel (originating from the 14th century) built in the middle of its grassy caldera, and the Croscat volcano, which has a cross-section cut away as the result of mining excavations. The area was designated a Parc only in 1985, after heavy lobbying to stop the volcanoes being destroyed by mining companies. The walking is very straightforward and the route is marked clearly with signs all the way round. On your return, ask to sample some of the *fesols de Santa Pau* (speciality beans) as part of your evening meal.

THE 11TH-CENTURY BRIDGE SPANNING
THE RIVER FLUVIA AT BESALU

Day 6: Santa Pau to La Miana
17.7 km (11 miles), 5 hours

Leaving Santa Pau and following grassy tracks, you journey uphill past craggy peaks and waterfalls until you reach a high ridge with lovely views of the Sant Martí Valley and Santa Pau. Along the way, you pass the 13th-century church of Sant Martí and the 12th-century church of Sant Vicenç. The further you go, the more isolated you become. There are few houses around, virtually all abandoned, so it is important to bring all your food and water with you at the start of the day. It is also worth leaving early in the morning so that your long ascent to Pruans does not coincide with the heat of the midday sun. However, when you reach Pruans you will be left speechless by the views of the Pyrenees on one side and the coast on the other. In September, you can quench your thirst on blackberries and wild pomegranates, before you descend to the remote hamlet of La Miana where the English-run hotel in a converted 10th-century farmhouse, Can Jou, has a welcome swimming pool.

Day 7: La Miana to Besalú
11 km (7 miles), 3 hours

As you head down a dirt path away from La Miana you pass an open area of rock, known locally as the 'Bonsai Garden'; between the rock cracks you will find a typical selection of Mediterranean shrubs, perfectly formed but in miniature. Continuing down through oak and pine forests, you arrive at the medieval town of Besalú, with its striking 11th-century fortified bridge. There should be more than enough time for you to explore the town before settling down at the three-star hotel, Els Jardins de la Martana.

Day 8: Return to Barcelona

Contact: ATG Oxford
www.atg-oxford.co.uk
TEL: +44 (0)1 865 315 678
FAX: +44 (0)1 865 315 697

Venturing into the wilderness of Yellowstone National Park in south-west Wyoming is like stepping on to another planet. With its 890,340 hectares (2.2 million acres) filled with giant chasms, pink-hued canyons, rumbling mud holes, explosive geysers, bubbling hot springs, a waterfall that is twice as high as Niagara Falls, free-roaming wolves, bison, mountain goats and grizzly bears, it is without doubt nature's greatest adventure theme park.

- 8 days/7 nights
- Route rating: fairly strenuous
- Dates: from June to September

Yellowstone and Grand Teton National Parks, USA

For walkers it provides some of the most outstanding scenery in the world. Originally the home of the Sioux American Indians, it was turned into the world's first ever National Park in 1872 and is now a World Heritage Site. Situated on a broad volcanic plateau around 2,438 m (8,000 ft) above sea level, it is a geothermic wonderland, where over ten thousand thermal features gurgle and simmer against a backdrop that early explorers of the region initially thought was an earthly incarnation of hell. Nowadays, though no less impressive, the area is regarded with affection instead of terror, and most of the geysers have individual names, including the famous Old Faithful which delights spectators by spouting out a 45,000 litre (9,900 gallon) jet of hot water every 40 minutes.

Just south of Yellowstone lies Grand Teton National Park, dominated by the sawtooth summits of the Teton and Gros Ventre Ranges, which shoot up abruptly from flat plains to heights of 3,600 m (12,000 ft). Looking at their soaring, jagged silhouettes, it is hard to believe that these mountains (which sit on a 64 km/40 mile geological fault-line) were once more than 9,000 m (30,000 ft) below sea level. The park teems with wildlife, including moose, big horn sheep, bear and vast herds of elk. In mid-summer, the area turns into a multicoloured wonderland as millions of wildflowers burst into bloom; wandering through the lush forests and meadows you are likely to see yellow arnicas, pink phlox and red-berried fairy bells among many others. Without the dramatics of a restless earth bubbling below its surface, visiting Grand Teton is an altogether more peaceful, though no less awesome, experience than Yellowstone.

Much of the walking takes place at a fairly high altitude, so it is important that you acclimatize yourself slowly; drink lots of water and do not push yourself too hard in the early stages of this trip. In the summer months, the temperature in Yellowstone and the Tetons ranges from 21°C (70°F) to 27°C (80°F), and is ideal for walking. It can be chilly in the early mornings, however, so warm clothing is highly recommended.

OPAL POOL, MIDWAY GEYSER BASIN,

YELLOWSTONE NATIONAL PARK

Day 1: West Yellowstone

After flying into West Yellowstone Airport (only open from June to September) make your way to the Stage Coach Inn, at the western entrance of the park. This traditional hotel looks as if it has come straight from the set of a Wild West movie.

Day 2: Upper and Lower Geyser Basins
10.4 km (6½ miles), 4 hours

Warming up with a gentle walk around the Fountain Paint Pots and the Celestine Pool, you can see up to six geysers spurting merrily at the same time. After lunch beside the Firehole River, make your way along the paved trails to the Old Faithful area, where you move from one extraordinary thermal feature to another, accompanied all the way by wisps of steam and the constant sound of bubbling. To get the best views of the spectacular Old Faithful eruptions, follow the Observation Point Trail, which takes you to an elevated spot about 60 m (200 ft) above the geyser; as with all parts of Yellowstone, anything even mildly off the beaten track is considerably less crowded, and this vantage point is no exception. Other stars of the show along the Upper Geyser Basin include Anemone Geyser, which has an eruption cycle repeated every seven minutes, and Grand Geyser, which produces streams of water that shoot up out of the ground to a height of 60 m (200 ft). From here you can walk directly to the Old Faithful Inn, where you will stop for the night.

Day 3: Grand Canyon of the Yellowstone
14.5 km (9 miles), 5 hours

An hour-long drive takes you to one of the park's most significant features, the Grand Canyon of the Yellowstone. It is 32 km (20 miles) long and 1.2 km (¾ mile) wide, with sheer cliffs that drop down over 360 m (1,180 ft), with two thunderous waterfalls and, like the canyons of Arizona, its walls are stained red, yellow, orange and gold Unlike in Arizona, however, here thermal vents spout up at regular intervals among the fir trees, creating a decidedly other-worldly feel. As you walk along the Wapiti Trail you should be able to see ospreys, which nest high above. Joining Uncle Tom's Trail, you climb down 328 stairs to Inspiration Point, which provides incredible views over the Lower Falls and into the depths of the canyon. By the time you arrive back at the Old Faithful Inn, the crown jewel of the area's hotels with wonderful views of Old Faithful, you will be feeling utterly awe-struck.

Day 4: Drive to Colter Bay 1.5 hours;
Emma Matilda Lake Trail
18.7 km (11½ miles), 5 hours

The scenery changes dramatically as you drive south to Grand Teton National Park — huge, savage-faced mountains rise high into the sky, while thick forests and tranquil lakes characterize the lower ground. From Jackson Lake Lodge, with its 18 m (60 ft) windows and panoramic views, you soon reach the undulating trail that takes you round Emma Matilda Lake. Walking through dense Englemann spruce forest, remember that this is prime bear country, so be sure to make a lot of noise.

Day 5: Jenny Lake and Cascade Canyon
up to 22.4 km (14 miles), 6½ hours

After a short car journey to Jenny Lake, followed by a boat trip across the lake, you reach the mouth of Cascade Canyon. It's a steep 0.6 km (1 mile) hike up to Inspiration Point, but once you are there, there is a great view of Jenny Lake and the glacial moraine that formed it, as well as Jackson Hole. Continuing along Cascade Creek, a glacially rounded canyon, you come out into pasture land drowning in mountain bluebells, paintbrush daisies and dandelions. If you are feeling tired, it's fine to stop at any point and turn back, as this is a 'there-and-back' walk. If you want to carry on, you can keep going until you reach Lake Solitude at 2,700 m (9,000 ft). Once back at Jenny Lake, it's into the car again for a quick ride to the ski resort of Teton Village and the spoiling luxuries of the Snake River Lodge and Spa.

Day 6: Rendezvous Mountain
11.4 km (7 miles), 4 hours

An aerial tram ride from Teton Village takes you up 1,242 m (4,139 ft) to the top of Rendezvous Mountain at 3,135 m (10,450 ft). This is a geologically fascinating area, and hiring a local guide to highlight the most interesting features is essential. Following the trail to Granite Canyon, you pass through forests and wildflower-filled meadows. The views over three mountain ranges – the Grand Tetons, the Snake Mountains and the Gros Ventre Range – are simply stupendous. This is a short day's walking, leaving you with plenty of time to explore the Wild West town of Jackson, just down the hill from Teton Village. The people of Jackson are particularly proud of their cowboy heritage – amateur shoot-outs are staged most week nights in the summer, and, after four-wheel drives, horses are the most popular form of transport.

SNAKE RIVER WITH THE GRAND TETONS IN THE DISTANCE

THE ANTELOPE FLATS BELOW THE GRAND TETONS

Day 7: Float trip down Snake River, 2 hours; optional afternoon walk

One of the best ways to see the wildlife in Grand Teton is afloat. Sitting on a watercraft as it silently glides downstream without disturbing any of the fauna (including moose, eagles and elk) that have come to the water's edge to drink and feed, you have the opportunity to observe the creatures' natural behaviour. The experience is almost spiritual as you watch the animals and gently soak up the views of the canyon from this new perspective. In the afternoon, if you are still feeling bouncy, you can take the tram from Teton Village and explore Rendezvous Mountain from a different angle, finishing the day off with a steep walk back down to the village. A massage in the spa at the Snake River Lodge is a perfect way to round off the trip.

Day 8: Depart Teton Village and return to West Yellowstone Airport

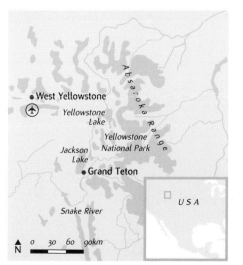

Contact: Backroads
www.backroads.com
TEL: +1 510 527 1555
FAX: +1 510 527 1444

If someone gave you a large dose of LSD and asked you to paint an imaginary landscape, you might come up with something similar to the canyons of Zion and Bryce in southern Utah. But, these extraordinary natural freak shows are not the product of a fevered imagination — they are the result of millions of years of erosion and tectonic plate movements.

- Route rating: moderate—fairly strenuous
- 8 days/7 nights
- Dates: May to October

Utah – Zion and Bryce National Parks, USA

Of the two, Zion National Park has the greater diversity — sheer, multicoloured sandstone walls, riverine forests, rugged peaks, breathtaking waterfalls and perilous chasms. It has such extremes of altitude, 1,117–2,618 m (3,666–8,726 ft) that a wealth of flora and fauna exists within its boundaries, including pocket gophers, bank beavers (so called because they don't build dams) and mountain lions. Over 800 species of plant have been found, ranging from cactus and yucca in the arid areas to ferns and box elders by the Virgin River, which runs along the bottom of Zion Canyon. For much of the year the river looks fairly benign, and it is hard to believe that such a meagre ribbon of water could be responsible for carving out the massive cliffs that tower above it. However, after heavy rain or snow-melt, the river becomes swollen with huge quantities of mud and sand: each year it carries away more than ten million kilograms (one million tons) of rock waste from the area.

It's almost impossible to give an accurate description of Bryce National Park. Even the Paiute Indians, who hunted in the area for many generations, couldn't find a quick way to sum it up, and just called it *Unkatimpe-wa-Wince-Pockich* which roughly translates as 'red rocks standing like men in a bowl-shaped recess'. Filled with *hoodoos* (pinnacles of rock, usually with large boulders balanced on the top), it isn't actually a canyon at all, but rather a row of crescent-shaped amphitheatres which rise up to 2,700 m (9,000 ft) above sea level. Its limestone and siltstone walls are stained red, white, orange, yellow, brown and even green by the high concentration of mineral deposits contained within them. This psychedelic fairyland is populated by mule-deer, chipmunks and ground squirrels.

Summer temperatures in both Zion and Bryce can rise to uncomfortable levels, so the best time to visit for a walking holiday is in May/June and late September when it is warm but not unbearably hot. Ironically, despite being deemed an arid zone, afternoon thunderstorms are relatively common, so waterproof clothing is essential. The other important factor to remember is that the combination of strenuous exercise, high altitude and warm temperatures can quickly lead to heatstroke and dehydration if you are not careful. Drinking several litres of water each day should ensure you avoid any unscheduled hallucinogenic experiences.

THE VERTIGINOUS ANGEL'S LANDING IN ZION NATIONAL PARK

Day 1: St George

The Mormon town of St George, southern Utah's largest metropolis, lies below a long sandstone escarpment. It is a 2-hour drive from Macaroon International Airport in Las Vegas and is the most convenient place to stay en route to Zion National Park. There are over 36 motels in the town, but one of the most enjoyable places to stay is the St George Resort & Spa, where you can indulge yourself with shiatsu or reflexology before the trip begins.

Day 2: St George to Zion National Park, 50-minute drive; Watchman Trail 4.8 km (3 miles), 2 hours

The drive from St George to Zion National Park is filled with dramatic scenery which becomes increasingly impressive, until you round the final corner into Springdale (the last town before entering the park) and are met with the awesome view of Zion Canyon. Leaving your luggage at the luxurious Desert Pearl Inn, you then make your way into the park for a warm-up hike. Where you go depends on the weather, but if it is not too hot the Watchman Trail is the most attractive and least crowded option. Climbing 110 m (368 ft) to the base of the Watchman formation, you are treated to the sight of the lower Zion Canyon, the Towers of the Virgin and the West Temple formations.

If the heat is too oppressive, you can choose the much easier Pa'rus Trail, 5.6 km (3½ miles) – the only downside to this is that it isn't enormously adventurous (it's suitable for wheelchairs right the way round) and is usually packed with other visitors. Returning to the Desert Pearl Inn in Springdale, your home for the next three nights, you can relax in the swimming pool next to the tree-lined river.

Day 3: Observation Point Trail
13.2 km (8 miles), 5 hours

There is a challenging morning's walk
ahead of you as you climb over 610 m
(2,000 ft) in the space of 6.4 km (4 miles).
But, keeping the mantra 'no pain, no gain'
floating in the back of your mind, you can
rest assured that the views along the way
and at the top are stunning. If you don't
feel up to such exertion, however, you can
take yourself off on a self-guided nature
trail to Weeping Rock, where you will find
a series of cliffside springs and a hanging
garden of ferns and wildflowers.

Day 4: Scout's Lookout and Angel's
Landing 14 km (8½ miles), 6 hours

After passing through the cool environment
of the aptly named Refrigerator Canyon,
you make your way up to Scout's Lookout
via a series of zigzags called Walter's
Wiggles. Once at the top, it's a good idea
to stop for lunch before you attempt the
challenging trail up to Angel's Landing.
With a sheer 450 m (1,500 ft) drop on
either side of the narrow track for the last
0.8km (½ mile) to the top, this is definitely
not to be tried by anyone who suffers
from vertigo. Chains have been bolted in
along the route for extra security, and
most people use them as an aid to haul
themselves up. Terrifying as it sounds,
walkers of all ages complete this trail,
and watching climbers ascend the north
face of Angel's Landing makes you realize
you've taken the easy route!

Day 5: Drive to Bryce Canyon, 2 hours; Fairyland Loop 15.8 km (10 miles), 5½ hours

Beautiful as the journey from Zion to Bryce Canyon National Park undoubtedly is, it doesn't do anything to prepare you for the surreal sights that surround you as soon as you enter Bryce Canyon. Weird geological shapes — spires, towers, natural hanging bridges, minarets — seem to sprout out from every angle, with a colour scheme that looks as if someone has spilled the contents of a paint palette over the whole place. The little-travelled Fairyland Loop takes you down into Fairyland Canyon, past hundreds of strangely shaped *hoodoos* and bizarre rock formations such as Tower Bridge. You climb the Chinese Wall, an ascent of 270 m (900 ft), and come out at the top of the canyon near Sunrise Point. Following the Rim Trail back to Fairyland Point, you pass juniper bushes and Douglas firs. There is only one place to stay in the park and that is the Bryce Canyon Lodge, spectacularly placed 90 m (300 ft) from the rim between Sunset and Sunrise Points.

HOODOO ROCK FORMATIONS IN BRYCE CANYON

Day 6: Queen's Garden, Peek-a-Boo Loop and Navajo Loop 12 km (7½ miles), 4½ hours

Descending the trail from Sunrise Point down to the basin known as Queen's Garden (owing to a *hoodoo* that is said to bear a passing resemblance to Queen Victoria), you wind between endless limestone fins and spurs. Once you have made it to the top of Peek-a-Boo Loop you will be rewarded with views ranging as far away as Canaan Mountain and the Kaiparowits Plateau. If you are still feeling energetic, the Navajo Loop travels to the bottom of the canyon again, 156 m (512 ft), but takes you past the huge Towers of Wall Street, as well as some of the most outlandish *hoodoos* in Bryce, including the enormous Thor's Hammer. Return to Bryce Canyon Lodge.

Day 7: Sheep Creek Trail 8 km (5 miles), 3½ hours

Walking for 1.6 km (1 mile) along the rim of the canyon, you have fabulous 360-degree views until you drop down the pink limestone cliffs to the canyon floor. Once there you make your way to Dixie National Forest, passing wide green meadows as you go. On the way back, if you have the time and the energy, you can follow the Under the Rim Trail as it meanders along the eastern side of the canyon, providing you with more surreal vistas — after which you will fully agree with the frequently quoted words of Ebenezer Bryce, the first European settler in the area: 'It's a helluva place to lose a cow!'. And for the final night, it is back to Bryce Canyon Lodge.

Day 8: Return to Las Vegas

SAFFRON COLOURED ROCK IN ZION NATIONAL PARK

Contact: Backroads
www.backroads.com
TEL: +1 510 527 1555
FAX: +1 510 527 1444

Index of walking companies

Numbers after walks indicate page references

Picture credits

The publisher would like to thank the following photographers, agencies and organisations for their kind permission to reproduce the photographs in this book:

4 Layne Kennedy/Corbis

6 David Hunter/ Robert Harding

8 Ed Cooper/Camera Press

9 Stuart Westmorland/Corbis

10 David Muench/Corbis

11 James Marshall/Corbis

12 David Muench/Corbis

13 Brandon D. Cole/Corbis

14–15 Paul A. Souders/ Corbis

16 Galen Rowell/Corbis

17 Yann Arthus-Bertrand/Corbis

18–19 Paul A. Souders/Corbis

20 Richard During/ Gettyone Stone

21 Michael Melford/ Gettyone Stone

22 Ronald Badkin/Travel Ink

23 Hans Peter Merten/Robert Harding

24 Paul Hardy/Corbis

25 Pictures Colour Library

26–28 Michael S. Lewis/Corbis

29 Robert Holmes/Corbis

30 Raymond Gehman/Corbis

31 left Brian McGilloway/ Robert Holmes Photography

31 right Paul A. Souders/Corbis

32 Derreck Furlong/ Robert Harding

34–35 Brian McGilloway/ Robert Holmes Photography

36 William J. Hebert/Gettyone Stone

37 Brian McGilloway/Robert Holmes Photography

38 Paul Felix/Collections

40 Barry Davies/Eye Ubiquitous

41 Roy Rainford/ Robert Harding

42 Gena Davies/ Collections

43 Chris Stock/Travel Ink

44 David Martyn Hughes/Images of France

45 Andrew Cowin/Travel Ink

46 Michael Buselle/Robert Harding

47 Andrew Cowin/Travel Ink

48 David Hughes/Robert Harding

49 Ron Chapman/James Davis Worldwide

50 Terry Harris

52 Adam Van Bunnens/Eye Ubiquitous

53 left courtesy of ATG Oxford

53 right Julia Waterlow/Eye Ubiquitous

54 Terry Harris; 55 Yiorgos Nikiteas/Eye Ubiquitous

56 Andrew Cowin/Travel Ink

57 Bob Krist/Corbis

58 N.A. Callow/Robert Harding

59 Pictures Colour Library

60 Hans Peter Merten/Robert Harding

61 Stephen Studd/Gettyone Stone

62 Jon Hicks/James Davis Worldwide

63 Pictures Colour Library

64 Karoki Lewis/Axiom Photographic Agency

65 Somendra Singh/DPL/Link India

66 Tony Gervis/Robert Harding

67 Chris Prior/Travel Ink

68 Viren Desai/DPL/Link India

70 Chris Gibb/Eye Ubiquitous

71 DPL/Link India

72 Ian Cumming/Axiom Photographic Agency

73 Chris Gibb/Eye Ubiquitous

74 Dallas and John Heaton/Corbis

75 Bruce Lowe;Eye Ubiquitous/Corbis

76 Richard Ashworth/Robert Harding

77 Tony Gervis/Robert Harding

78 D. South/Camera Press

79 Gavin Hellier/Robert Harding

80 Paul Thompson/Eye Ubiquitous

81 Pictures Colour Library

82 John Heseltine

83 Nick Bonetti/Eye Ubiquitous

84 courtesy of ATG Oxford

85 Pictures Colour Library

86 Micheal Diggin/Collections

87 Van Parys Media/Camera Press

88 Roy Rainford/Robert Harding

89 Paul Thompson/Eye Ubiquitous

90 Simon Harris/Robert Harding

91 Jon Millen

92 JNTO Image Library

94 Tibor Bognar/Corbis

95 Tom Stanley; 96 JNTO Image Library

97 left Tom Stanley; 97 right JNTO Image Library

98 David Keith Jones/Images of Africa Photobank

99 Christophe Bluntzer/Impact

100 Tim Davis/Gettyone Stone

101 David Keith Jones/Images of Africa Photobank

102 Jorn Stj Erneklar/Impact

103 Pictures Colour Library

104 Jon Millen

105 James Davis/James Davis Worldwide

106–107 Jon Millen

108 Chris Caldicott/Axiom Photographic Agency

109 Pictures Colour Library

110 George H.H. Huey/Corbis

111 Adam Woolfitt/Robert Harding

112 George H.H. Huey/Corbis

113 Roberto Gerometta/Robert Holmes Photography

114–115 David Muench/Corbis

116 Dallas and John Heaton/Corbis

117 Dominic Harcourt Webster/Robert Harding

118 Robert Knight/James Davis Worldwide

119 Thierry Bouzac/Impact

120 Dominic Harcourt Webster/Robert Harding

121 James Davis/James Davis Worldwide

122 Mike Mcqueen/Impact

123 Dennis Barnes/Collections

124–125 Mike McQueen/Impact

126 Kathy Collins/Robert Harding

127 Mike McQueen/Impact

128 William Gray/Travel Ink

129–130 @nher; 131 Tony Arruza/Corbis

132 left Jose Fuste Raga/Corbis

132 right and 133 @nher

134 Chris Caldicott/Axiom Photographic Agency

135 Michael Busselle/Robert Harding

136 P. Higgins/Robert Harding

138 M.Allwood Coppin/Eye Ubiquitous

139 Peter Kingsford/Eye Ubiquitous

140 Ramon Fortia i Rius

141 courtesy of ATG Oxford

142–143 Harriet Scaramella/courtesy of ATG Oxford

144 Ramon Fortia i Rius

145 Graham Lawrence/Robert Harding

146 M. Winch/Axiom Photographic Agency

147 Laurence Fordyce/Eye Ubiquitous

148 Mary Winch/Axiom Photographic Agency

149 Geoff Renner/Robert Harding

150 Roy Rainford/Robert Harding

151 Mary Winch/Axiom Photographic Agency

152 J.Sparshatt

153 Tony Gervis/Robert Harding

154 Jon Hicks/James Davis Worldwide

155 left Geoff Renner/Robert Harding

155 right and 156 J.Sparshatt

157 Jon Hicks/James Davis Worldwide

Every effort has been made to trace the copyright holders for photographs. We apologise in advance for an unintentional omission and would be pleased to insert the appropriate acknowledgment in any subsequent edition.

Author's Acknowledgements

With grateful thanks to the team at Conran Octopus – Katey Day, Sian Lloyd, Sybella Marlow, Jeremy Tilston and Catharine Snow. Equal thanks go to Jon Millen, Hugh Arbuthnott, Adam Hopkins, Julie Snyder, Aline Keuroghlian, Vanessa Buxton, James Harper and Janet Goldby.